inner.
magic

inner. magic

a guide to witchcraft

Ann-Marie Gallagher

BARRON'S

First edition for the United States, its territories and dependencies, and Canada published by Barron's Educational Series, Inc., in 2001.

First published in Great Britain in 2001 by Mitchell Beazley, under the title *Inner Magic*, an imprint of Octopus Publishing Group Ltd
2–4 Heron Quays, Docklands, London E14 4JP

All inquiries should be addressed to:
Barron's Educational Series, Inc.
250 Wireless Boulevard
Hauppauge, New York 11788
http://www.barronseduc.com

International Standard Book No.: 0-7641-1919-2

Library of Congress Catalog Card No.: 2001090181

Printed in China

9 8 7 6 5 4 3 2 1

c o n t e n t s

This book is about what witches believe and what we do. It explains the spiritual and magical dimensions of witchcraft, and offers an opportunity to experience some of these. It is also a celebration of a spiritual path whose time has come. Witchcraft is a nature religion whose followers are city dwellers; it is a path that honors intuition in an age of science, and is a movement that values interconnection in societies where rampant individualism is the norm. Its roots and inspirations lie in the ancient past but its spirit is always in the present with its face turned toward the future. Witchcraft embraces and makes sense of these apparent contradictions through its ethical and responsible practices. Witchcraft is a real-world spirituality.

Witchcraft is a spiritual path and a way of life. It embraces a reverence for nature, the practice of magic, and a desire for change. The starting point for effecting change is within ourselves; thus this book is called *Inner Magic*. Changes do not only take place from within but this is the place from which we begin. Witches see all existence as a great web, with all things interconnected, so inner magic is also outer magic. Yet we have to start somewhere and as a wise man once said, "The journey of a thousand miles begins with a single step."

growth of modern witchcraft

Witches are ordinary women and men who choose to follow a spiritual path that connects us with the cycles of nature. We are highly passionate about keeping alive old pagan traditions and exploring how these traditions are relevant to us today. Our pagan spirituality links us to both an historical and reconstructed pre-Christian era of goddess worship, and we see all aspects of nature as sacred.

Witchcraft's current popularity is due to several converging factors in its recent history. After the repeal of the Witchcraft Act in 1951, Gerald Gardner, a practicing witch, published a book on the secret craft of witches. Wicca, Gardner's version of witchcraft, is a spiritual and magical system based on ancient religions that appealed to many who were dissatisfied with more established religions. At the same time, increased awareness about the condition of the environment led to an interest in alternative lifestyles, particularly spiritualities that revered nature and rejected doctrine. For many people, Wicca answered these needs as it is a spirituality that reveres nature and planet earth as sacred. Wicca also incorporates roles for priestesses and reveres a goddess as well as a god, and this was the basis of its attraction for many women. Although the women's movement was strong and widespread in the 1970s in Britain, it was in the United States that feminism became truly incorporated into Wicca.

Witches' beliefs differ among the varying types of witchcraft. However, generally we give priority to "the goddess," who incorporates the male and female. The goddess is considered the source of all existence and we are also part of the goddess ourselves.

the craft

Witches celebrate the seasons, consciously try to grow and change, and work magic for ourselves and others. The type of witchcraft described in this book is typical of several different approaches to what we call "the Craft". The Craft is a closely related mix of spiritual and magical practices, and most witches would have difficulty separating the two completely. Our magical practices are so much a part of our spirituality that it is necessary first to understand something of our beliefs and practices before describing how we do magic. This, therefore, is a book of two halves: The first half concentrates on spirituality, practices, and finding your spiritual path; the second half is concerned with spellwork and rituals.

building magical skills

It is very tempting to skip to the back of the book straight to the spells, especially if the possibility of performing spells and magic is quite new to you. However, the making of magic and the path of a witch are much more than this, and the success of spellwork depends on developing a working understanding of how the web of magic operates. This requires you to absorb new information, build new magical skills, and develop a sense of your own personal history. The first half of this book opens up these possibilities and offers guidance, information, exercises, and frameworks for you to build upon as you progress along the path.

In the course of the last forty years, alongside the growth of interest in the environment, there has been a general move toward a more organic type of religion. For many, especially women, this spiritual quest has been influenced by feminist ideals about women's social equality and an interest in alternative and complementary healing, many aspects of which cross over into the realm of alternative spiritualities.

The current interest in magic is shown by the vogue for myth and enchantment in popular culture. Many television programs such as *Sabrina the Teenage Witch*, *Charmed*, *Buffy the Vampire Slayer*, and *Xena: Warrior Princess*, significantly all with strong female characters, are enjoying huge popularity. It is not surprising, then, that witchcraft, sometimes described as a nature religion, offering women prominent roles as priestesses, is an obvious spiritual home for people searching for something more than what is offered in more orthodox religions.

The principles of witchcraft are relatively simple: The *Wiccan Rede*, by which witches measure the consequences of their actions states: "*An it harm none, do thy will.*" This means that, although we are free to choose how we act, we must ensure that our choices do not harm anyone. In a spiritual path that honors nature as sacred and sees spirit in all things, this is often extended to include nonhuman life. Many witches interpret harming none to imply all living things. For some, this means becoming vegetarian; for others, who place trees, rocks, plants, and even planet within the category of "none," it means protecting the earth by recycling, planting, and campaigning to prevent environmental destruction. What appears to be a very simple rule is in fact at the center of a responsible and ethical philosophy. Witchcraft is a joyful, positive spiritual path.

The following principles apply to most types of witchcraft and are generally recognized among witches.

web of life

Witches see all existence as an infinite, interconnecting web of life. This concept is significant in relation to the principles of witchcraft and its warning to "harm none." If we see ourselves as part of the web, and as weavers of it, then it becomes impossible to remove ourselves from the things that we do and the values that we act upon. If one part of the web is shaken, the whole web trembles.

The principle of interconnection is particularly strong in witchcraft, and our spiritual and magical development depends upon our understanding of it. This principle does not flatten our individuality, but stresses the need for it to be balanced by acknowledging our interdependence with others. Learning our place in the world is part of our pagan spirituality. Exploring and reconnecting with nature also involves working out where we are in relation to the rest of the world.

body and spirit

Another valuable aspect of seeing the universe as a web is that it encourages us to reverse the separation between mind, body, and spirit that has evolved in the West over the last two thousand years. This separation, which elevates rationality and science over intuition and everyday experience, is seen in witchcraft as artificial and damaging. Our spirits are not separate from, or better than, our bodies, and significantly, our bodies are considered sacred as part of nature and of the goddess.

spells for personal gain

It is not thought selfish in witchcraft to perform spells or rituals for yourself. We believe that valuing ourselves helps us to value others. Self-sacrifice for its own sake is not encouraged in witchcraft. The desire to help people should arise out of a sense of our dependence on each other, and the realization that we are all part of the same web. Therefore, casting a spell when we are in need, or getting friends to help us to regain balance after trauma in a ritual is seen as a healthy activity.

Casting a spell for material things, for ourselves or for others, is also acceptable in witchcraft. It tends to work best if it is a genuine need; casting spells on a whim is to be avoided. You should respect the energies you work with and use common sense regarding what you are expecting. There is never any "price to pay" when requesting things for ourselves or others through magic. Witches do not believe in providence or demons, so we don't make "deals."

the circle

The major site of the spiritual and magical business of witchcraft is the circle. This is often referred to as "the" circle because all circles are considered to be part of a single, eternal circle. Casting a circle is described later in this book, but it is important to know the reasons for doing so. A circle is made from energy that is raised and directed out, usually through one person, into the air surrounding a ritual space, and is visualized as light. Walls and floors do not present obstacles to this kind of energy, so a circle can be cast all around a room by someone standing in the center. The space within the circle is described as being "between the worlds." This signals its uniqueness as a place of communion and connection, since it provides a corridor between our desires and their outcomes. Significantly, time does seem to pass differently when you are in the circle; it is common to emerge from what was imagined to be an hour spent in the circle, only to find that three hours have passed.

festivals and celebrations

The shape of the witch's year is marked by Esbats and Sabbats. Esbats are full-moon celebrations, most commonly kept by covens and now generally referred to as "full-moon" circles. Sabbats are the eight great festivals of the year, divided by some commentators into the Greater Sabbats, which are the four fire festivals, and the Lesser Sabbats, which are the solstices and equinoxes. In practice, however, these are all now regarded as equally important.

extraordinary journey

In the course of this book, you will be introduced to a number of concepts, beliefs, ideas, and journeys. You will also explore the importance of the seasons and the cycles of the earth, moon, and sun. You will discover what it is to be a witch. This book proceeds on the understanding that you are interested in witchcraft, but it does not assume that you wish to be initiated or that you have extraordinary powers. However, it is true to say that everyone is extraordinary in some way; it is now up to you to discover which type of extraordinary person you are.

the eight festivals

Witches stay connected with the cycle of the seasons by marking the changes we see all around us throughout the year. Our pagan spirituality provides us with traditions reaching back over hundreds of years and it inspires us to create some new ones. The witch's calendar consists of eight major pagan festivals or Sabbats: Samhain (pron: "Sah-wayne") or Halloween, October 31st; Yule or Winter Solstice, December 21st; Imbolc (pron: "Im-bulk") or Brighid (pron: "Breed"), February 1st; Eostre (pron: "Eestah") or Spring Equinox, March 21st; Beltane, May 1st; Litha or Summer Solstice, June 21st; Lughnasadh (pron: "Loo-na-sah") or Lammas, August 1st; and Mabon or Autumnal Equinox, September 21st.

timing of festivals

These festivals are a mixture of fixed astronomical events represented by the solstices and equinoxes, and Celtic fire festivals, which are slightly more moveable feasts. The two "sets" of festivals broadly relate to solar and seasonal events. The dates given for the solstices and equinoxes are approximate as, in some years, the actual solstice or equinox falls just outside the date, but they are physical events that can be predicted in advance. The dates given here for the Celtic fire festivals—Imbolc, Beltane, Lughnasadh, and Samhain—are those most widely recognized by the pagan community. However, some people prefer to shift them toward seasonal changes, which differ from year to year. Imbolc, for example, marks in part the awakening of the earth from the winter. Accordingly, some pagans like to wait until the first snowflakes emerge before celebrating this festival. Similarly, Samhain marks the beginning of winter, and although this feast is widely recognized as falling on October 31st, some pagans elect to celebrate when the first overnight frosts arrive.

Some of these revivals of old festivals contain a good deal of modern inventiveness. The majority of the festivals named above cannot be traced back through documentation much before 1100. This is not surprising, as written documentation specifically describing pagan customs prior to 1100 is quite rare. The solstice and equinox celebrations do bear echoes of ancient observations of the heavens, as seen in the alignment of many prehistoric sites with specific solar, lunar, and sidereal events. Surviving folk traditions associated with different times of the year also support a history of honoring the seasons in a way different from those laid down by the Church or State. However, historical verification is considered less important than what the festivals mean to us now, and the way in which we are able to connect the past, present, and future within our celebrations.

christianity

It is intriguing that many Christian festivals occur on or around the pagan Sabbats. Christmas, for example, is just after the Winter Solstice and Easter is on the first Sunday following the full moon after the Spring Equinox. Some commentators claim that modern pagans have appropriated some of these festivals and this has been a matter of some debate. However, it is odd that the two most important festivals of the Christian year, Christmas and Easter, occur respectively, near to the rebirth of the Sun on December 21st, and the lengthening of the days (known as "Lent"), to the triumph of light at the Spring Equinox. Many pagans prefer the explanation that a new incoming religion appropriated and redefined the old festivals, in the same way that some churches were built over pagan sites in order to tempt the populace into church.

star child

Depending on which tradition a witch follows, the cycle of the year can also tell a story. For witches who follow the god/goddess tradition, there are key points in the year that represent their courtship, mating, conception, and birth-giving roles. Yule is when the goddess gives birth to the star child, and at Imbolc the goddess is a young maiden again. The star child is conceived at Eostre and the god and goddess then marry at Beltane. At Litha, the god reaches the height of his powers, only later to fade and be sacrificed as John Barleycorn in the harvest at Lughnasadh. The goddess mourns him through Modron, which is the end of summer. She then visits him in the land of the dead at Samhain, and finally gives birth to him/his son again at Yule. For more goddess-centered pagans, the shape of the year may be seen as an ongoing spiral of death and rebirth. This spiral is, in turn, linked with women's life cycles and the passing of roles among daughter, mother, and grandmother. Others prefer to simply see the festivals as natural markers of the passing seasons, and a reason to come together and celebrate the deeper meanings of our passage through the solar year.

eight-spoked wheel

The most common concept of the witch's year is an eight-spoked wheel, with each spoke representing a festival. We can be said to fasten onto these spokes as the wheel turns in order to connect with the cyclical changes taking place around and within us. The following descriptions of the festivals will introduce you to some of the many traditions and origins of this "wheel," and its present-day meaning for modern witches.

samhain

The feast of Samhain ("Sah-wayne") takes place in the fall, when the leaves fall from the trees and the greenery of summer diminishes. As the first frosts of winter appear and the fruits of harvest have gone, pagans remember their beloved dead and honor their ancestors. There are a number of historical precedents for associating this time of year with death. Records dating from 730 C.E. (Common Era) tell us that November was known as "Blod-monath" (Blood Month), the time when beasts were selected for slaughter before winter. From around the 8th century, the Christian church in northern Europe remembered its early martyrs on November 1st, thus firmly setting a cultural association with death at this time of year.

halloween

Samhain is recognized as "Halloween" in the Northern Hemisphere, and is the festival most popularly associated with witches. In stores throughout England, Scotland, Wales, Ireland, and the United States, masks of elderly green-skinned crones, black pointy hats, and fake broomsticks go on sale. "Punky night" as it is sometimes called, is renowned as a time when mischievous spirits are abroad, some in the shape of small children who knock at doors demanding "treats" in exchange for immunity from "tricks." Although popular images of witches at Halloween emphasize the "old," "ugly," and "wicked" stereotype, the frightening elements of these images do reflect something of what Samhain means to witches.

the crone

Samhain is the season of death, and is associated with the Hag, the old, wise aspect of the goddess. At this time she is the Washer at the Ford, who prepares shrouds for the dead, and the midwife who receives us at the end of life when we are reborn into the Otherworld. The Calliach, Carlin, or Crone aspect of the goddess is not an easy aspect to assimilate and celebrate. She represents a frightening facet of our existence—the certainty of death. She is the Old One who rules over our passage into the dark side of the year, as well as our passage into the unknown realm of death. The appearance of the Hag in the form of ugly masks at Halloween bears a close relationship to what witches celebrate at Samhain: the fact of decay, old age, and eventual demise. Our society does not value old age highly, particularly in women. However, for those of us who revere the Crone aspect of the goddess, old age is not necessarily equated with ugliness, but with experience, wisdom, and accepting death as part of the cycle of life.

It is a tradition that, on the feast of Samhain, the veil between the worlds of the living and the dead is much thinner than usual. In reality, the thinning of this boundary is created from within ourselves: it is because the dead are so much in our thoughts at the dying of the year that the boundaries between life and death appear to dissolve, and allow us to commune with the past.

honoring the dead

Witches usually celebrate Samhain by having a circle, either alone or with other witches, to celebrate the passage into the dark side of the year, and to honor those who have died during the year since the last Samhain. We invite the spirits of those who crossed over during the last lunar year into our circle, which is traditionally opened in the west, the quarter of death, and leave a spare place when the bread and ale is shared at the end of the ritual. Different traditions celebrate in different ways, and the ritual can vary from year to year. It is usual to remember the past summer and say good-bye to the warmer, lighter days. It is common to name those who have died in the past year before moving on to others we wish to commemorate. This can be an emotional affair and it is an accepted part of the ritual that people use this occasion to grieve, weep, and talk to those who have died. When all the greetings and farewells have been said, those who have been born since last Samhain are welcomed by name, and new things that have come into people's lives since last Samhain are acknowledged. The practice of grieving for what is gone, then celebrating what has come turns the energies around and confirms the continuous nature of existence. This is sometimes called "the Spiral Dance," and some covens perform this dance to symbolize the constant cycle of death and rebirth.

celebrating "punky night"

Many witches are more than happy to throw themselves into the more public forms of celebration by throwing Halloween parties, making scary pumpkin heads, and joining in the nonsense of the night. Pagans see the popular association of Halloween with ghosts and monsters as a healthy acknowledgment of human fears about darkness, nightmares, and our relationship with the dead. It is entirely in keeping with other aspects of our festival to participate in the more garish celebrations of the season, as well as honoring its more serious side as the Day of the Dead and the beginning of winter.

yule

The Winter Solstice provides a wonderful opportunity for a festival of light to brighten up the dreary midwinter. Usually known as the shortest day, December 21st is also known as "sun return," and "mother night" in honor of the goddess who has given birth to a new solar cycle. It seems likely that this latter feast name has been appropriated by Christians and pagans to commemorate either the goddess or Madonna giving birth, although which came first is inconclusive. However, whatever the origins of the festival, the physical event of the shortest day provides its key focus. On this day, pagans throughout the Northern Hemisphere choose to celebrate the death of the old solar year and the "rebirth" of the new. The festival's other title, "Yule," comes from the Scandinavian name for festivities held during the midwinter period.

standing still

Although modern-day pagans tend to cite Samhain as the Celtic New Year, there is a strong case for claiming Yule as the beginning of a new year instead, as it marks the beginning and end of the earth's solar cycle. Pausing in the darkness of winter to consider what has passed and what may come seems to be a natural psychological element of the festivities. The word "Solstice" is actually derived from the Latin "Sol stice" or "sun stands still." Pagans use the darker half of the year positively, as a time to rest and grow psychologically and spiritually. The festivities at midwinter give us a chance to mark the darkest, shortest day, look back to the year that is gone, and look forward hopefully to spring and summer.

greenery

For witches, deep winter is a time to celebrate our spiritual relationship with the seasons of the earth, and to bring light and hope out of darkness. We decorate our homes with evergreens, including holly for protection, ivy for constancy, and mistletoe for fertility. Bringing greenery into the home in the middle of the winter symbolizes the presence of life, even when all around seems barren in the depths of winter. Each solar festival can be said to carry the seeds of its own destruction. At Summer Solstice, the longest day, the days thereafter grow shorter and the sun's power is diminished. At Yule, the shortest day, the opposite is true. The shortest day, therefore, is emphasized as a time when the sun's strength will hitherto increase, in spite of the fact that it is also the time when we experience the longest night.

light within darkness

Yule can be celebrated in a circle with other members of a coven or alone. The theme of light in darkness is emphasized and it is usual for the ritual to incorporate the lighting of candles around the ritual space. Solar and star symbols dominate, alongside the ubiquitous greenery at this time of year. Pagans incorporate a number of old traditions into the solstice celebrations, including a Wassail cup, or communal drink of alcoholic punch or mulled wine. The expression "wassail" comes from the Anglo-Saxon "Waes Hael," meaning "Good health." Alongside the custom of going a-wassailing or enjoying your neighbors' hospitality, is the giving of gifts at this time of year. Whether the exchange of gifts originated from those given by the Magi to the infant Jesus, or whether it derives from a much earlier Roman pagan feast, this period is traditionally marked by generosity and hospitality. Some witches even like to exchange small gifts in the Solstice circle. These gifts are, in a sense, true gifts, that do not need to be reciprocated. Occasionally, these gifts are symbolic ones, the members of the group writing down wishes anonymously, to be distributed by lottery among the group. A wish in this case might be in the form of one word that describes something to help us get through the winter, for example, "friendship," "laughter," or even "chocolate." This midwinter festival is marked a few days later by the festivities of Christmas and many pagan families like to combine these two events, distributing some gifts at Solstice and further gifts at Christmas.

contemplation in darkness

Yule is a time for contemplation in darkness, then celebration in feasting to light up the darkness and encourage the rebirth of the sun. Witches use the dark and light aspects of the Winter Solstice to reaffirm their connection with the cycle of the year, and to confirm their spiritual path within the paradox of light within darkness. The midwinter festival is a joyful time, that affords witches a chance to celebrate with friends.

imbolc

Imbolc (pron: "Im-bulk"), sometimes known as Brighid (pron: "Breed"), is a Celtic fire festival, marking the "quickening" of the earth in preparation for the spring. The first snowflakes emerge around this time, and in northern Europe, where the festival originated, it is known as the lambing season. The word "Imbolc" comes from the Old Irish, and is thought to mean "Ewes' milk," indicating how closely this feast was linked with new birth. Over time, this popular festival, dedicated to the triple goddess Brighid, has seen both Christian and pagan traditions incorporated into its celebrations. Stories and traditions of the goddess Brighid and the Irish Saint Brigit have become conflated over time and it is often difficult to differentiate between them. Today, pagans celebrate Imbolc as the season of new growth and as the feast of Brighid.

guardian of the oppressed

Witches revere Brighid in her traditional role as a goddess of metalworking, poetry, and healing, and in her more modern role as a strong and fierce protector of women. Feminist witches honor Brighid as an independent goddess who is a friend to the oppressed and, for this reason, she is celebrated as a guardian of children (especially newborns), animals, and vulnerable people in society. Historically, Brighid was a goddess of learning and healing, and there are many healing wells named after her in England, Ireland, and Scotland. Myths and customs concerning Brighid abound throughout these places, and there is a rich seam of tradition regarding her importance to women. In the Isle of Man she is known as either Breeshey or Vreeshey (pron: "vree-shah"). Today, there are still in existence women's songs in the Manx language inviting Brighid into the home. The connection between the goddess Brighid as midwife to the spring, and Saint Brigit as midwife to Jesus are reflected in the celebrations; Imbolc is very much a women's festival.

bridiog

When pagans and witches celebrate in mixed groups, it is customary for the men to be excluded from the early part of the circle. During this time, the women perform a short ritual for Brighid, which is never revealed to the men. The men traditionally pay a forfeit or carry a gift for Brighid before they are allowed to enter the circle. Often, there is a "Bridiog" prepared. This is a doll representing the goddess, who reclines in a basket or cradle, and is decorated with jewelry, often with a brooch or pin placed over her heart. The doll then presides over the feast. In the course of the celebrations, people are allowed to approach the doll and whisper secrets to her, or ask her to grant wishes, leaving little gifts of food, drink, and beads by her side.

the maiden

The Christian version of this festival, Candlemas, lends another tradition to the pagan celebrations—that of exchanging candles as gifts or lighting many white candles in the ritual space. The flower of the festival is the snowdrop, and some witches like to make chaplets from the flowers for the candles, or make ringlets for the women to wear in their hair. Imbolc celebrates the "Maiden" aspect of the goddess. This does not imply virginity, but independence, freshness, and youth, and the festival of Imbolc reminds us to discover these attributes within ourselves. As we get older, it is easy to get jaded and skeptical. Imbolc is the time to regain enthusiasm, declare our independence, and fight for social and political change. Some women choose to light candles at this time to symbolize the personal changes they will experience in the coming year.

awakening the land

The role of Brighid as a goddess of fire is highlighted at Imbolc. When the sun begins to melt the frosts of winter, witches imagine Brighid breathing on the sleeping land to awaken the first green shoots. As patron of smiths, specifically metalworkers, Brighid's fiery aspect is seen as transformative; as patron of poets, she is seen as the spark of inspiration. Her third role, as patron of healers, means that if any spellwork is done in the Imbolc circle, it is usually in response to requests for healing. In line with her role as protector of the oppressed, an Imbolc circle might also include spells to grant energy for new projects, or to strengthen the resolve of those working for social justice.

Imbolc gives witches the opportunity to appreciate the changes taking place in nature as winter loses its grip and new life emerges. It also offers us a chance to reignite our spirit and desire for justice in the world, as well as rediscover the sparks of youth and freshness within.

eostre

Eostre (pron: "Eestah"), also known to witches as "Ostara," falls at the Spring Equinox when day and night are of equal length. It is the time when we celebrate spring and mark the beginning of the lighter days. Eostre celebrates the balance of light and darkness, and the new growth evident all around us. Other names for Eostre are "Vernal Equinox," or "Festival of Trees," both of which stress the seasonal spread of greenery.

the hare

The name of this festival is probably derived from that of a European goddess of fertility or beginnings, known as "Eastre" or "Eos." She is today strongly associated with an animal totem, the hare. Some pagans, notably goddess-centered and feminist witches, honor the goddess Andraste at this time as she is recorded in ancient Roman annals as the deity to which Boudicea released a hare prior to battle. Little else is known of this divine figure and she has been assigned as an earth goddess, whose symbol, the hare, is seen to frolic in the fields at this time of year. Accordingly, the image of the Easter bunny on greeting cards and the array of chocolate bunnies at this time is regarded with great fondness by witches.

eggs and fertility

Eggs have been associated with this time of year for centuries. As many birds nest around this time, it is natural that the fertility aspect of the festival has come to be symbolized by an egg. The giving of eggs in spring has origins going back over 800 years, and records of the custom are found throughout Europe and in parts of Asia. More conservative observers place the origins of this tradition within early Christianity, but given the nature symbolism of the egg as life in potential, pagans prefer to claim ancient, pre-Christian origins for it. Some witches celebrate by decorating the circle with painted egg shells, or giving little gifts of sugar or chocolate eggs to participants at the end of the Eostre ritual.

eostre wishes

This time of year is marked by an abundance of wild flowers with patches of daffodils appearing in northern Europe. The crocuses form blankets of white, saffron, and purple on the forest floors, while fruit trees are laden with white and pink blossom. Spring flowers are used to decorate the Eostre circle to represent the new life occurring in nature, and to symbolize the growth we must seek as individuals and as part of our communities. The flower of this festival is the yellow daffodil. A popular way to celebrate the festival is to echo the Christmas custom of hanging baubles on a tree. This is done by decorating a fallen branch and dressing it with "wishes" for the time between Eostre and Modron, the Autumnal Equinox. The branch is secured in a vase or pot, and decorated with flowers, ribbons, hanging crystals, painted egg-shells, patches of needlework, and other symbols of things that we want to grow during this time. This brightens the ritual space and enables participants to hang wishes for seasonal growth on an "Easter tree."

balance and growth

While the days are lengthening and the sap is rising, witches also think about human growth and the projects that we wish to see "blossom." The balance between night and day at the equinox inspires us to look within and around us, to identify where there is imbalance in our lives, our health, our attitudes, and to seek to rectify this. In the circle, we seek balance in our own lives, and endeavor to bring harmony to the world around us. In order to symbolize this, some witches light one black candle and one white. This reminds us that we stand between the light and the dark in perfect balance prior to entering the new phase of the solar year. It also reflects back to us our various responsibilities in seeking balance in our way of life.

Eostre is the time for putting winter behind us and clearing the way for new growth, psychologically and physically. The custom of spring cleaning provides an opportunity to get rid of clutter, things we have outgrown or no longer need. It is also a good time to decorate our living spaces and reflect the beauty blossoming in nature.

beltane

The Celtic fire festival of Beltane signals the beginning of summer and celebrates fertility and marriage. The improved weather enables Beltane celebrations to take place outdoors, among the greenery that characterizes the festival. The increase in warmth and the coming of days that are significantly longer than the nights make this a solar-based festival. It is also a time of carnival, excess, and high spirits, and is associated with fairies and nature spirits at play.

trickery and teasing

Witches see Beltane as a time when the veil between the worlds is much thinner than usual. Just as at Samhain, when the separation between the living and the dead is breached, Beltane is traditionally a time when you can be led astray in the woods by the antics of mischievous "feys," or the magic of the "Sidhe" (pron: "Shee") people: the magical race who live in the hillsides of Ireland. Whether or not one believes in "fairies" as actual entities or simply as a metaphor for fertile nature, Beltane is undoubtedly a time of exuberance, trickery, and teasing.

love chase

The more sexual side of Beltane, commemorated on village greens with phallic maypoles topped with yonic circles of flowers, has engendered some quaint customs involving games and chases. The tradition of young men and women going into the woods at sundown on April 30th and emerging on the morning of May 1st, having "gathered in the May," indicates an element of license in sexual matters. One notable Beltane game involves the chasing of consenting women by men carrying a "randy pole" with which they try to touch the women. The sexual and phallic nature of this love chase has, in the 20th century, earned the public disapproval of the Church. In modern times, the festival has also become associated with the Morris, thought, accurately or not, to be latterday renditions of ancient fertility dances. Some Morris sides still dance at dawn on May 1st to encourage the sun to rise, thus combining the fertility and solar aspects of the festival. Throughout history, attempts have been made to ban the popular May Day celebrations. It is interesting to note that this popular "people's festival" was chosen in the 19th century as the day on which to commemorate the international struggle for workers' rights. It seems somehow fitting that ordinary working people should choose a day that has been the bane of authority and the joy of the masses for many centuries.

sun-god

The origin of the word "Beltane" is taken from the name of a sun-god known in northern Europe and less so in Britain, as "Bel" or "Belenos." Goddess-centered pagans have a counterpart for Bel in the lesser-known goddess "Belissama." Their names, meaning "shining," make it likely that they are both stellar or solar deities, and Roman references to Bel as the "British Apollo" confirm this link. The second part of the word "Beltane" links it clearly to "tine" or fire. Records dating from over a thousand years ago speak of cattle being driven between "Bel-fires" to protect them from pests before they were put out to pasture. Given the reference to a pagan god or goddess, and the fact that the early written records refer to this as an already established custom, pagans seem justified in claiming the festival as genuinely pre-Christian.

celebrating beltane

If at all possible, witches prefer to celebrate Beltane out of doors. Communal bonfires at nightfall are a popular element of celebrations, as are maypoles, which are usually more modest than the gigantic ones that appear on village greens. As this is a popular time for pagan weddings, or "witches' hitches," as they are somewhat irreverently dubbed, Beltane is traditionally a time to make promises and commitments. One way of symbolizing this is to jump over a broomstick as one makes a promise. This is also the crucial part of the handfasting ceremony that seals a couple's commitment to each other. It is also a popular time for mimicking the old games associated with "Maying" and sexual license by tying bells on some participants, giving them a head start, and sending the rest of the coven to find them. The reward for successfully catching a belled "hare" is a kiss for the "hound" in question! Another popular game for a Beltane gathering is to "pair up" unwitting guests by randomly placing the name of a divine couple, i.e., Aphrodite and Aries, Shiva and Kali, or even Zeus and Ganymede, on their back. Each person tries to discover his/her divine identity by asking other guests questions to elicit simple "yes" or "no" answers. They then have to set out to discover their allotted "partner."

At the end of the ceremony, covens or groups that are fortunate to have a large, communal cauldron have the option of jumping over a lucky Beltane fire, made from ignited alcohol and Epsom salts. This action helps summarize the joyful, wild character of Beltane, whose many traditions offer witches a number of delightful ways to bring in the summer.

litha

Litha is the festival celebrated at the Summer Solstice. For a few days in midsummer, as at midwinter, the sun is seen to "stand still," as it sets in the same place for the few days of the midsummer period. The physical solstice usually takes place on June 21st. On June 20th, pagans often set out before darkness to keep vigil all night and welcome the sunrise at dawn on the longest day. Just as the Winter Solstice marks the shortest day and the rebirth of the sun, the Summer Solstice marks the longest day and the downfall of the sun. For witches, this is a time to celebrate the height of the sun's powers, and an opportunity to gather strength just before the days become shorter over the following six months.

midsummer fires

The origins of the name "Litha" are obscure, but it is thought to mean "wheel." This is in keeping with the old custom, recorded over the last two thousand years, of rolling a fiery wheel down a hillside at midsummer. This act celebrated the strength and fall of the sun. Significantly, cheese-rolling traditions still take place around villages in England at this time of year, although it is not known whether there is a direct correlation between these and the custom of wheel rolling. Litha, like Beltane, is associated with fire, and bonfires and torches lit at this time are found in written records from 700 years ago. The fire aspect seems to have strong connections with a form of folk magic, representing like with like, to encourage the sun to rise up on the day of its greatest trial. Historically, the midsummer fires have, like the Maying customs, been subject to attempted overthrow in the last five centuries, most notably by the Church authorities. Like Beltane, midsummer encouraged people to stay up all night, kindling the suspicion of licentious behavior, and it was strongly linked in the eyes of the Church with pagan, and later Catholic, ritual.

drawing energy

The period just prior to and after Litha is noted in the pagan community as a time when progress in different areas of life seems, like the sun, to reach a standstill. Witches tend to deal with the occasional lassitude that besets covens around Litha by drawing upon the solar energy now reaching its peak, and recharging our spiritual and physical "batteries." This is achieved by visiting the sites where the solstice is celebrated publicly, sitting and absorbing the warmth of the sun on the longest day, and engaging in guided visualizations that facilitate the assimilation of solar energy. We psychologically "store up" the energy raised at midsummer so that we can draw on it to take us through the remainder of the summer and into the dark again. One popular charm to invoke the strength of the sun involves using a red thread to tie four matchsticks together in an eight-spoked wheel, to be worn around the neck or hung above the bed on a ribbon until the Autumn Equinox. The live matches, representing the fires of the sun, can be lit one by one during this period to release energy to you as you need it. Safety precautions regarding this charm cannot be stressed enough.

unity

Today, it is common to celebrate the Summer Solstice outdoors at stone circles, on hillsides, and at locations where there is a clear view of the midsummer sunrise. In this way, we get to meet others celebrating the longest day and experience the energy-enhancing experience when hundreds of people greet the sunrise together. The custom of an all-night vigil around a bonfire can be a wonderful experience, and community singing, storytelling, and the sharing of food and drink throughout the night are important parts of the long wait for dawn.

The festival of Litha offers opportunities to gather energy from the rising power of the sun, and to share in the community of the fireside. For those of us who keep vigil alone through the shortest night, it is moving to know that as we do so and greet the sunrise, thousands of people are doing the same thing, at exactly the same time.

lughnasadh

Lughnasadh (pron: "Loo-na-sah"), sometimes known as "Lammas," is the celebration of the corn harvest. The name of this feast originates from Ireland, and it is connected with the god Lugh, with whom present-day pagans associate the sun. Lughnasadh relates directly to a cereal, rather than any other type of crop, such as wheat. It marks the ripening and gathering in of grains and the sacrifice of the corn for the good of the people. Although Lughnasadh is considered to be one of the Celtic fire festivals, its origins outside Ireland and the Isle of Man point to an Anglo-Saxon feast on August 1st. It is probable, however, that the feast of "loaf mass" or "Lammas" was the continuation of an ancient British agrarian custom.

corn dolls

There are many myths and customs associated with this festival, providing a rich cache of traditions for pagans to draw upon. First, there is the cutting down of "John Barleycorn," seen variously as the god who married the goddess at Beltane or as an aspect of the goddess who scythes off part of her earth body in order to feed her children. Records from the 19th century describe a custom that ensured that the poor of the parish were admitted to a field directly after the cutters left, to "glean" all grains that were not attached to a stalk. In this way, the poor could legitimately participate in celebrating the "first fruits" of the harvest with the rest of the community having enough grain to bake their own bread. One of the most familiar customs associated with the harvest is the making of corn "dolls," thought originally to have been woven to capture the spirit of the corn. This was to ensure that abundance did not flee from the community with the gathering of the harvest. The contemporary practice of hanging corn dolls in the house for good luck is a continuation of the sympathetic magic once practiced to trick the corn spirit into remaining all year-round.

poppy wedding

The poppies that appear in the fields around this time are sometimes referred to by pagans as "Blood on the Corn," linking the harvest with the theme of sacrifice. Another interpretation is that of bright poppies arising in celebration of the harvest. This celebratory aspect of poppies is reflected in the custom of the "Poppy Wedding," still celebrated in Lancashire, England as recently as the 1980s. According to this tradition, brides who wed at harvesttime wear red and carry a sheaf of corn in place of the usual floral bouquet; their headdresses and other adornments are also woven from corn.

spiritual and material wealth

Witches see Lughnasadh as a time for celebrating the good things in our lives, and remembering how much we physically depend upon the earth for our food. Witches revere the earth as sacred and are aware of the environmental damage from pollution and irresponsible farming methods that can compromise nature's balance and future harvests. We also acknowledge the social injustices that occur as some people prosper and others starve. Lughnasadh is about harvest and distribution. The theme of fairness is particularly potent at a time when we are celebrating our own good luck. Accordingly, some witches combine the themes of plenty and sharing by enjoying the ritual feasting, and volunteering time or money to charitable work.

thanksgiving

Lughnasadh is best celebrated with others: a communal meal is usually part of the celebration. A Lammas loaf baked in the shape of a ringed braid or a sheaf of corn is commonly shared at the feast. Lughnasadh rituals include a thanksgiving element, with each person expressing their gratitude for the good things that have come to them in the past year. As this festival also provides an opportunity to separate the wheat from the chaff, metaphorically speaking, it is a good time to symbolically cast away those things that are no longer needed. A common way of distributing blessings in the circle is for each person to weave or tie up a bundle of corn or hay, and attach a gift tag with the blessing that they are commemorating written upon it. This is then passed on to someone else in the circle as an extra gift for them to take home with them from the harvest.

Lughnasadh is for gathering in, sharing, and acknowledging our spiritual and material wealth. It is also a time to consider what we might do to ensure that future harvests are uncontaminated and equally distributed.

modron, (mabon)

Modron (Mabon), or the Autumn Equinox, stands, like Eostre, at a midpoint between the dark and light halves of the solar year. Whereas the Spring Equinox heralds longer hours of daylight, Modron prefaces longer hours of darkness. In the wheel of the year, conceived as a compass, the Autumnal Equinox stands in the west. In the British Isles, this is the site of the great Atlantic Ocean and the place of the sunset. British ancestors believed the souls of the dead were transported westward over the water to the Summerlands or the Land of Eternal Youth. Modron, like Eostre, is a time of balance, but it is also seen as the time when the light dies and summer ends.

mother

This time of year sees many fruit harvests, and Modron, meaning "mother," celebrates the fruitful earth before the trees grow bare again and we descend once more into winter. At this point in the cycle, the term "mother" refers to the ripening fruits and to the mythological goddess, mother of the star child, who at this point in the year is entering her seventh month of pregnancy. However, just as fertile nature ripens, the days shorten and the trees prepare to shed their leaves. The myth that is most popular in ritual circles at this time is that of Persephone, daughter of the earth goddess Demeter, who descends to the underworld. While she is there, she eats six pomegranate seeds and is bound to return there for six months of each year to keep company with the dead. In Persephone's absence, Demeter, the earth goddess, mourns for her daughter and allows the trees and plants to wither and die. When Persephone returns in the spring, Demeter decorates the earth with flowers and greenery to honor her return. Many rituals for Modron involve the eating of pomegranate seeds so that we, like Persephone, are prepared as we enter the dark of the year.

avalon

Modron also has connections with the Arthurian cycle of legends. The legendary King Arthur was said to have been borne away at his death by three maidens, representing the triple goddess of the land. They carried him by boat across the western ocean toward the sunset, to be healed in the Summerlands. Witches who incorporate the Arthurian cycle into their belief system see Arthur as a semidivine aspect of the solar god wedded to the earth goddess. For them, the descent of the sun at the Autumn Equinox is symbolized through Arthur's departure into the west at his death, where he awaits rebirth as the star child at Yule. Another aspect of Arthurian legend commemorated at this festival is the concept of Avalon, a floating Otherworld, also known as the Isle of Apples. Apples are eaten by witches in Modron rituals to remind us that we walk "between the worlds" of the everyday and the imaginary, the past and the future, the mundane and the fantastic, in perfect balance. The apples are cut horizontally to expose the five-pointed star at their core: symbol of the five elements of life, and of spirit, which joins all things together.

farewell to the light

There are echoes of the harvest celebrations in Modron rituals, which often involve using acorns or other seeds to symbolize projects or wishes that we hope to materialize the following summer. The ritual space at Modron is usually decorated with fallen leaves, along with the fruits, nuts, and seeds to be found at this time of year. If it is warm enough to celebrate outside, near a river or the sea, some witches participate in a "Viking funeral." This entails floating a model boat, usually made of paper or boxwood, and setting it alight as it drifts away. This gives the dying sun a proper pagan funeral. A more modest version is to float lighted beeswax votive candles out onto the water in tiny paper "boats," taking care not to be near any brush, chanting or singing a farewell to the light.

Modron is a festival of balance and provides a chance for us to bid farewell to the summer. The fruits and seeds of the harvest used to symbolize our wishes for the following summer are entrusted to the deep earth to germinate during the darkness of fall and winter.

This festival completes the cycle, bringing us back to the feast of Samhain.

cycles of the sun

The eight festivals represent the major markers or "spokes" in the wheel of the year. These festivals provide a map by which we can track the progress of the earth's annual passage around the sun. However, there are other aspects of the solar cycle that are used by witches to develop intuitive and creative abilities, and to aid physical and psychological balance.

The solstices and equinoxes have already highlighted the importance of light and darkness in the cycle of the festivals. Although the balance between them shifts backward and forward in unending flow, there are discernible points in the year where one predominates over the other. The light and dark halves of the year run between the Spring and Autumn Equinoxes, at which points hours of darkness and light are momentarily equalled. After the Spring Equinox, the days grow longer until the sun reaches its zenith at the Summer Solstice. The days then begin to shrink back until day and night are of equal length again at the Autumn Equinox. After the Autumn Equinox, the opposite occurs.

using the cycle

Witches use this cycle to good effect, both physically, psychologically, and spiritually. As we work so closely with the cycle of the seasons, we take care to time our projects in accordance with the energies within and around us at different times. The light half of the year is seen as the ideal time for projects to be put into action, along with carrying out more energetic tasks, traveling, and getting outdoors. The dark half of the year is felt to be better for conserving strength, looking inward, contemplating, generating, and nurturing our creative and intuitive faculties. The dark half of the year is also ideal for planting the ideas that will hopefully come to their fruition during the lighter part of the year.

Physically and psychologically, this cycle makes perfect sense. Trying to galvanize people into action in the darker half of the year, when energy levels are low, is generally a waste of time. Similarly, expecting to be inward-looking, meditative, and still in spring, when the sap is rising, is bound to lead only to disappointment. However, there are deeper energies at work here, and witches work with these energies as part of the imperative to work with, rather than against nature. These energies have a variety of theories attached to them, but most witches agree that different times of the solar year generate them, and that the most obvious divisions are the points between the solstices and the equinoxes.

different concepts of time

In terms of spirituality, some witches claim that the lighter part of the year lends us a different sense of time than the darker half. The concept of time in the light half of the year is sequential, linear, and forward-progressing. In contrast, the sense of time that develops in the darker time of the year is cyclical, accumulative, and nonlinear. If these different concepts of time were described in terms of thinking, thought associated with the light half would be logical and rational, whereas thought associated with the dark half would be lateral and intuitive. Although this division sounds suspiciously like the sexist divisions made between masculine and feminine, there is a great deal to be said for it. It is logical for a different sense of time to develop in us in winter, when more time is spent indoors and light and energy levels are low. This period allows us to explore our inner being, and can give rise to an associative, cyclical way of thinking, during which time passes more quickly than we think it does. Witches also note how, in the darker part of the year, dreams are often stranger, more vivid, and even prophetic than in the lighter half of the year. In the lighter half of the year, when we are more energized, our thinking is more ordered. Accordingly, our sense of time is likely to be more organized in a straightforward, linear sequence.

festivals and time

The time between Samhain and Yule is particularly good for exploring and developing our psychic and magical powers, while Yule to Imbolc is a good time to keep a dream diary. Beltane to Lughnasadh is a time to commune with the spirits of the greenwood, which are part of the fey or faerie world, while Lughnasadh to Samhain is the best time for shedding sadness or other burdens. The time between Imbolc and Beltane is perfect for personal growth, setting one's health in order, and gathering energy from the lengthening days.

When you become used to working with the elements of air, fire, water, and earth, you will notice how differently you relate to them at various times of the year. In summer the element of air is encountered in the open spaces we visit, fire in the light and heat of the sun, water as the seas, rivers, and pools we swim in, and earth as the grass, rocks, or sand we sit on. In winter, air is the wind that howls outside our homes, fire is a welcome source of heat, earth is good, hot food to nourish and sustain us through the cold, and water is a hot bath or shower after a wintry day.

Sensing how the energies change over the course of the solar year is a key part of developing our spiritual and magical selves.

cycles of the moon

The lunar cycle is highly important to witches. We time our rituals, spellwork, and many of our celebrations to the appropriate phase of the moon, and we work hard to attune ourselves to its cycle. Later on in this book, you will be introduced to the magical principles linked with the phases of the moon. However, the moon's cycle has a spiritual and psychic importance in witchcraft that goes beyond the purely magical uses with which it is most popularly connected.

mirror of the soul

In the tarot, an ancient system of archetypes and symbols, the moon represents psychic power, dreams, emotions, illusion, and a capacity for self-deceit. These meanings are acknowledged to a certain extent within witchcraft, as the moon is seen as a mirror of the soul. As patron of dreams, which reflect our true feelings and desires, the moon is able to reveal what we hide from ourselves, and strips us bare of pretension and social restraints. Historically, people who stayed too long in the moon were believed to suffer madness, and were classed as "lunatics" a word that comes directly from the Latin for "moon." Today, witches, who occasionally dance beneath the moon, do not become deranged in its presence, but use it as a symbol of hope for those who try to work outside society's constraints. To work with the moon is to discover more subtle forms of power. Witches do not exert control over others, but become empowered within themselves, and this is often described as "power within." The moon's cycle, which is more frequent, immediate, and visible than that of the sun, reflects the constant changes in our lives. Witches use this cycle to frame our spiritual practices, and to hold circles at different phases of the moon—most notably coming together in groups at full moons or Esbats.

crescents and full moons

The first crescent in the moon's cycle is dedicated to Artemis, the moon goddess. This is a time for decision making, new projects, and moving forward. The last crescent of the moon's cycle is sometimes known as "Sickle Moon" and is dedicated to Hecate, the triple moon goddess in her old, reaper aspect. This is a time for cutting away and severing things that are no longer needed in our lives. Full moon, a time of fruition and completeness, is generally given over to a celebration of life's mysteries and in raising energy for healing ourselves and others. The different moons in the year also have names and associations, although these vary between traditions. The full moons at

Beltane and Samhain are thought to be particularly potent. Going into the circle to meditate and commune with the gods and/or goddesses at Beltane or Samhain can produce some powerful visualizations that can help us to develop spiritually and magically.

women and the moon

The moon keeps the same face turned to us as it rotates around the earth and so the patterns on its surface have become familiar to humankind throughout the ages. The tendency of humans to arrange random patterns into familiar ones has led us to interpret these markings, and those of the crescent moon, as a human face. Not surprisingly, humans have tended to have a more personal relationship with the moon, our closest celestial neighbor, than with any other heavenly body. The ancients carried this relationship over into the realm of human fertility and tended to have more moon fertility goddesses than gods. This is perhaps partly because of the association of the lunar cycle with women's menstrual cycles. In a world that timed things by the position of the sun and the seasons, pregnancies were timed in moons, leading to a link between childbirth and female fertility. The patterns on the surface of a full moon can also be seen to resemble a baby in the womb, something that would not have been overlooked by our fertility-conscious ancestors. The moon, therefore, is often referred to as female and has, in magic, more than a passing relationship to matters of menstruation, the female life cycle, and pregnancy.

psychic power

For witches, the cycle of the moon represents the changes in our life cycle, and its energies help us to attune to and realize our true desires. Dream diaries help us to note the different types of dream we experience in accordance with the different moon phases. Witches consider the moon's psychic effect on humans to be as powerful as its physical ability to produce tides in the great oceans. In witchcraft, the power of the moon is no less than that of the sun. On the contrary, the subtlety of the moon's energy is considered to be the most valuable single aid to developing our magical abilities.

gods and goddesses

Not all witches are pagans since not all witches worship the earth, and not all pagans are witches. Paganism refers to a collection of spiritual paths, of which witchcraft is one. These spiritualities revere nature as sacred, and draw upon ancient and not-so-ancient traditions to energize and inform their spiritual practices. Witchcraft draws upon pagan beliefs both for inspiration, and to draw a line between the past and the present. One of the key ways we do this is through our reverence of ancient pagan gods and goddesses.

one as many

Witches' beliefs regarding their gods and goddesses differ significantly from those of any other world religion. Our relationship with, and concept of god/dess is quite unique, and comes partly from the fact that we tend to see One as Many and vice versa. For example, there is no conflict between honoring many goddesses, as they are all part of the Great Goddess. However, not all gods and goddesses are the same. Pagans are able to celebrate many god/desses as well as referring to the Great God/dess.

Witches are able to accommodate a great deal of diversity, and this can be seen in the way that we differ in which deities we honor. Some witches celebrate the goddess only, as they believe that, just as the words "goddess" and "female" contain the words "god" and "male," so the goddess includes divine aspects of both male and female. Others regard these as two halves of the same divine power, but try to keep this concept separate from the sexism invoked by the terms "masculine" and "feminine."

the god

The god is seen as the son and consort of the goddess, and is regarded as being supportive in his strength rather than dominant. He is sometimes revered as the Green Man, the wild spirit of fertile nature. At other times, he is seen in the solar cycle as the Child of Promise, Impetuous Youth, and Mature Consort. In this cycle, his strength begins to fade at Litha and he is cut down as John Barleycorn at Lughnasadh. Sometimes witches refer to him as Cernunoss or Herne the Horned God, but as many witches note, he is not really "horned" but "antlered."

maiden, mother, and crone

The goddess is seen in many different aspects, as a Mother Goddess, as source of all life, as patron of fertility, as compassionate, as fierce protector, and as the source of wisdom. Most witches recognize her triple aspects of "Maiden," "Mother," and "Crone," all descriptions that are shorthand for independence and autonomy, passion and nurture, and experience and connectedness. The Maiden aspect of the goddess has nothing to do with sexual experience, it simply emphasizes the fierce and joyful spirit of independence. Goddesses associated with this aspect include Athene, Brighid, Bloddweuth, Diana, Maia, and Persephone. The Mother aspect of the goddess not only suggests fertility, pregnancy, birth, and nurture but also worldly experience, and liberated sexuality independent from pregnancy and parenting. Goddesses of love and fertility include Aphrodite, Astarte, Demeter, Gaia, Isis, Juno, Laxmi, and Rhiannon. The Crone aspect of the goddess celebrates the wisdom that comes with age, and the connections between birth and death. These include the goddesses Cailliach, Ceridwen, Hecate (pron: "Heck-a-tee"), Kali, Lilith, and the Morrigan.

equals

Witches see god/desses as friends, confidants, and supporters. We do not see our god/desses as abstract figures that punish or reward. Rather, we see them as within and around us, integral parts of our existence. Some witches see the figures of the god/desses as symbolic rather than as real entities, and enjoy being able to identify their belief system through them. Other witches see the god/desses as entities in their own right, which through the millennia have developed personalities because of the strength and nature of human belief. Others believe that the god/desses have always been here, because we cannot conceive of them in any other way.

We call upon our god/desses to help us in our spiritual and magical work. However we believe in them, they help inspire us to grow, to understand, and to change the world around us, and to lend their power to ours when we cast spells. We see our god/desses as equals and as part of ourselves.

The beliefs and practices of contemporary witches bear little resemblance to some of the myths attached to us. In addition to the largely obsolete iconography of the "wicked witch" in fairy tales, there are fears about where witches get their power, and what they are prepared to offer in return. This lack of understanding has led to some odd beliefs about witches.

One of the most common charges against present-day witches is that we worship the Devil and work to bring evil into the world. Witches neither believe in the Devil, which is a Christian concept, nor subscribe to "good" or "evil" as abstract notions, and so these accusations are somewhat misguided. However, as recently as in the 1990s, politically influential fundamentalist Christian organizations have tried to persuade the authorities that witches abuse or murder children. These claims have been made in the total absence of any evidence. That such groups can use the ages-old ruse of linking the target of their hatred—witches—with child abuse and murder is not very surprising. After all, our ancestors leveled similar accusations against Jews, heretics, gypsies, and gays. However, in an age that demands rational proof, it is interesting that they are often able to convince others that such a conspiracy exists.

This chapter examines the history of the witchcraft persecutions, and summarizes the main explanations offered by modern-day historians for the witch-hunts phenomenon. It will also look at popular images of witches in fairy tales past and present, and offer a brief resumé of witchcraft in folklore. Exploring the history of witchcraft in this way helps to explain how modern ultraconservative religious groups can persuade some members of the public that witches are evil and in league with the Devil. These very same witches vow to "harm none" and do not even believe in the Devil.

folk magic

Spell casters of great renown can be found throughout ancient mythologies. In the Egyptian pantheon, the goddess Isis reassembles and brings to life the dismembered body of her husband and brother, thereby casting the first spell. Ancient patriarchal Greece cast the Stygian witches—three sisters sharing a single eye between them—as loathsome and unpleasant creatures in the myth of Perseus and Andromeda. Some spell casters are portrayed as more beautiful but nonetheless perfidious. Some of the earliest witches recorded in Western history are characters from Homer's *Odyssey*. His hero Odysseus encounters a number of women on his journey homeward, including Circe and Calypso, both attributed with magical powers. Circe, who is specifically described

sorcery, folk magic, and witchcraft have a very long history. Most folk magic seems to have evolved from "sympathetic" magic

as a witch, turns Odysseus's men into swine before he tricks her and forces her to turn them back again to men. This ability to change bodies from human to animal form occurs thousands of years later in folk beliefs in northern Europe.

Sorcery, folk magic, and witchcraft have a very long history. Most folk magic seems to have evolved from "sympathetic" magic. This is a transference process by which a person or animal is represented by an object held by the spell caster. In times when hunting was important, this type of magic could be used for protection and good fortune in the hunt. Evidence left in caves and prehistoric sites strongly supports the case for "sympathetic magic" as an ancient practice. Paintings and other depictions of antlered figures suggest either a deity of hunting or the holding of magical rituals that acted out the hunt and its favored outcome before the hunters set out.

We know from the evidence collected by the Victorians that forms of sympathetic magic were present in folk medicine. This is particularly true of the famous medieval *Doctrine of Signatures* that held that the appearance of a plant had relevance to its medicinal properties. For example, the present-day use of St John's wort in overcoming depression was first applied in folk medicine because of the sunny color of its cheerful petals. Some types of folk magic overlap surprisingly accurately with the physical properties of some of the remedies known, tellingly, as "old wives' tales." For example, present-day use of aspirin as a painkiller stems from the use of willow bark, known as "witches' aspirin," as an analgesic. Digitalis, taken from foxgloves, was used by village herbalists to treat palpitations, and is still used in cardiac medicine today. The old practice of staunching a bleeding wound with spider's web is mentioned in Shakespeare's *A Midsummer Night's Dream*, and it was later discovered in the 19th century that webs contain a substance able to reduce temperatures. A number of plants, known as "woundworts" in honor of their power to aid the healing of cuts, have since been found to contain properties that speed coagulation of the blood and sterilize the wound. Some examples of "woundworts" are pimpernel, yarrow, comfrey, and valerian.

Other practices of folk magic used for cures are less directly attributable to the medicinal properties of the ingredients used. Instead, transference is the main principle. For example, it was believed for centuries that warts could be removed by rubbing them with a toad, thus transferring them to the creature itself. Other magical charms for the disposing of warts included rubbing a stone on the wart and tying it, with a live toad, inside a cloth that was then dropped in the middle of a pond. It was believed that this would again transfer the offending wart to the unfortunate toad, which

This typically negative depiction of two witches from the early 16th century shows them preparing a sinister magic brew.

a number of plants, known as "woundworts" in honor of their power to aid the healing of cuts, have since been found to contain properties that speed coagulation of the blood

would then drown. Another method involved rubbing the wart with two halves of a potato, which were then quickly joined together and buried. Alternatively, you could "nail" them by inserting a thorn or pin into the wart and then driving the thorn or pin into the earth or a tree.

The people approached for these "cures" were found in most villages. As well as being the source of magical advice, many cunning men and women had extensive herbal and anatomical knowledge. Knowledge of gynecology and midwifery in particular was handed down from mother or grandmother to daughter. These women would attend births, sit with the dying, and "lay out" the dead. They were attendants at the two most mysterious and important rites of passage undergone by humans. They also had knowledge of contraception, abortifacients, and aids to virility and fertility. Their knowledge of anatomy and medicine also favored them as animal doctors. At a time when whole villages depended on the milk and reproductive capacities of one or two beasts, the fate of an animal was crucial to the survival of the community. Expertise in animal and human well-being, therefore, was especially prized.

The attribution of such powers came to be double-edged by the time of the persecutions. However, as long as there was no one to gainsay the treatments a wise woman was dispensing, any failures to save a woman in labor, her child, or a sick animal could be explained as the will of God. When beliefs began to shift toward the conviction that witches were the Devil's agents, however, these wise women were automatically suspect, regardless of how helpful they had been to their community.

the folk magic and cunning lore of the wise woman or wise man were not necessarily linked with evil. Their services were valued in societies that depended upon such knowledge

Before that time, the folk magic and cunning lore of the wise woman or wise man were not necessarily linked with evil. Their services were valued in societies that depended upon such knowledge for survival. Early edicts to desist from witchcraft were mainly designed to stop the populace from participating in pagan rituals and return them to Christian ways, or to advise against belief in the supernatural power of witches.

This did not mean, however, that "bad" witches did not exist in the popular imagination before the 15th century. Although folktales of witches prior to this time included tales of those who were seen as beneficent, there was also a tradition of bad witches who caused harm. Witches could be held to be responsible for any ills that befell a community. If a cow fell ill after an unpopular person had cast her eye on it, then that person took the blame. There were a number of ways by which to identify the malefactor, all of which provide intriguing insights into beliefs about witches' abilities and powers. One popular way of identifying a culprit was to nail a suspected witch's footprint. This, of course, is a form of sympathetic magic in itself. The idea was to wait until the person, usually a woman, had passed by, and then, without her

beliefs held that witches could not cry more than three tears in succession, could not cross over running water, could not drown, and could not say the Lord's Prayer without choking

knowledge, drive an iron nail into her footprint left in the dust or mud. The witch was then identified by the fact that she would be seen limping. If damaging her footprint could damage the witch herself, this indicates a special relationship between the witch and her environment. This type of witch-hunting implies that witches are, in certain circumstances, susceptible to antimagical devices. The use of an iron nail is particularly telling, as it matches folk beliefs concerning iron and magic. It was believed that the fairy-folk could not abide the presence of iron, and so the proverbial horseshoe above the door of the house became a weapon to keep out supernatural forces. Later on, alleged witches were buried face down beneath an iron plate, or with their joints pierced with iron rivets to prevent them from rising from the grave. Similar beliefs held that witches could not cry more than three tears in succession, could not cross over running water, could not drown, and could not say the Lord's Prayer without choking. These beliefs imply that witches were held to be inherently magic, rather than simply casters of spells, a significant contrast to the later beliefs that were to creep in via the Catholic Church during the 15th century.

Other abilities attributed to witches included shape shifting. It was thought that witches could change themselves into different animals and run wild for a while before turning back into human form. Their favorite creatures of choice were hedgehogs, cats, and hares. One way of finding out if witches were abroad at night was to shoot at an animal you suspected of not being natural in its behavior. If the next day the suspected witch was ill, or infirm in the limb that was shot, she was a proven witch.

These folk beliefs were later to become enmeshed with a more dangerous and forcefully implemented system of beliefs about witches that emerged in the witchcraft persecutions of 15th-century Europe.

the persecutions

Witches all over the world refer to the period between 1500 and 1700 as "The Burning Times." This refers to the time when the persecution of alleged witches was at its height in Europe and spread to the New World of the Americas. During this period, hundreds of thousands of people, mostly women, were killed as a result of being prosecuted for alleged witchcraft. Although we should not assume that anyone accused of witchcraft automatically went to the fires, the practice of burning human beings alive as a result of "proven" witchcraft accusations still provides the most horrific image of this period. Most people approach this troubled period in history by asking why such violent persecutions came about. A number of explanations are offered, many of them seemingly contradictory. The truth may lie in the crossover between these theories, which point to a complex and diverse set of circumstances that led to the witch-hunts.

sexual, political, and economic upheavals

Europe between 1500 and 1550 was subject to rapid social, political, and economic upheavals. A sharp change occurred in the economic basis of social relations, and with this came the erosion of medieval ideas concerning charity and obligation toward the poor. A series of wars, famines, climactic changes in northern Europe, and the closing down of common and tenant farmers' lands created a larger poor and homeless population. These changes also produced a tension between the new elite, merchant-based, and growing capitalist classes, and the folk culture of the ordinary people. Increased centralization of the law made it possible for such tensions to be played out

"The Burning Times" of 1500–1700 saw the worst persecution of alleged witches—mainly women—in history.

on a legal basis. The new elite classes could hand over to the courts those they deemed to be "undesirable," or who placed their faith in folk customs that undermined secular or ecclesiastical authority. It was the provision of new laws that enabled the witchcraft persecutions to take place.

the evil of women

This period also saw a more repressive attitude developing toward women. A number of pamphlets published at this time

make it clear that women were to be subjugated and ruled, and any man who allowed otherwise was considered to be less than a man. During the transformation of the old economic bases, women were thrown out of the trades, and consequently were most subject to poverty and homelessness. There was also an increasing focus upon what could be called "sexual crimes," such as abortion, contraception, and infanticide. "Bastardy," another specifically female crime installed in some countries, meant that women found guilty of bearing a child outside marriage were subject to

during the transformation of the old economic bases, women were thrown out of the trades, and consequently were most subject to poverty and homelessness

imprisonment. This new emphasis on "policing" women's fertility and sexuality is highly significant: information about an accused witch's sexual reputation, and whether her behavior was "proper" and womanly, was to be an important part of some of the witch trials. Chauvinistic attitudes toward women were not new, but the violence with which these attitudes were pursued was quite remarkable. Some legal historians claim that this period saw, for the first time, the criminalization of women as a group.

In 1486 two German monks, Kramer and Sprenger, published the famous *Malleus Maleficarum* or *Hammer of the Witches*, which railed against the perfidy and evil of women. They were following Turtullian, an influential philosopher of the early church, who told women, "You are the Devil's gateway... How easily you destroyed man, the image of God. Because of the death which you brought upon us, even the Son of God had to die." However, Kramer and Sprenger went even further than this, extending the original sin of Eve to that of being easily persuaded by the Devil and being more naturally lustful than men. They claimed that "All witchcraft comes from carnal lust, which is in women insatiable." Witches, they claimed, were invariably women, who were weaker of resolve than men, and who could conjure men's strength away from them. Their book contained fantastic tales of events that the monks claimed to have witnessed themselves, including one of witches conjuring away men's members and depositing them in nests, where they lived like birds. These bizarre ramblings incorporated beliefs that were already familiar to their readership: the weakness of women and their "natural" tendency toward evil. Receiving the full authority of the Church, and sanctioned by Pope Innocent VIII, the

Malleus Maleficarum became highly influential. It was virtually a torturer's handbook, including advice on what to look for in body searches, and how to question an accused witch.

diabolical compact

The belief that witches made a pact with the Devil, known as the "diabolical compact," became popular in the 15th century. During the next two centuries, all accused witches were seen as doing the Devil's work. At a time when the Church saw people's souls as more important than their bodies, the reaction to those believed to be doing the Devil's bidding was extreme and punishments severe. Being tortured for the good of the soul was seen by the clergy as broadly acceptable. Torture was tolerated when the sufferings of the body were as nothing compared to the torments faced by sinners in the afterlife.

The "diabolical compact" saw witches as doing the Devil's work. This medieval woodcut depicts witches and the Devil riding together on broomsticks.

torture and murder

In 1532 Charles V, the Holy Roman Emperor, extended the use of torture on suspected witches to imperial law. Consequently, Germany saw mass trials and burnings throughout the 16th and 17th centuries. As torture was used to extract the names of other witches from the accused, the list of alleged witches grew with each prosecution. This period in Germany saw accusations spread throughout entire communities, thus confirming the authorities' belief that witchcraft was a widespread conspiracy rather than the dabblings of the odd midwife or wise woman. Changes in the law in countries all over Europe now saw all forms of magic as evil. All witches were seen as minions of the Evil One, to whom they allegedly swore oaths and danced with at orgies known as "Sabbats." In some countries the slightest suspicion could condemn the unfortunate to the torturer's hands. On rare occasions, the families of accused witches did receive compensation for loss of work due to infirmities caused by the torture of the innocent. However, the nature of the torture often ensured that the victim confessed. Torture by the boot, which crushed the feet, ankles, and lower leg, and the pilliwinks, or

thumbscrews, often forced the accused to confess to anything to end the torment. Retractions could mean repeated torture, and records show that many victims confessed in order to avoid further torture before their inevitable death, as well as to save their families from implication in their alleged crime.

The widespread use of torture in the Holy Roman Empire to secure confessions and the denunciation of others as witches resulted in the decimation of families. In Germany, professional witchfinders were employed by communities to find witches among them, and both secular and religious authorities confiscated land from wealthy families who were found guilty of witchcraft. This aspect of the witch-hunt is perhaps the easiest to explain, witchcraft beliefs and the machinery of the law enabled avaricious individuals and organizations to condemn their victims and claim their wealth for their own. This was straightforward murder and theft. The psychological aspect of witchcraft accusations is perhaps more difficult to comprehend. It is tempting to apply our present understandings of human psychology to these accusations, but this was a very different period from ours in many respects.

Innocence did not always mean protection from death. This woman is being dunked in the water to try her innocence. Only if she drowns, is she proven not to be a witch.

That witchcraft beliefs were genuine is without question; there are cases where family members would accuse each other from a true belief in the diabolical compact. Tragically, one German Prince, Philip von Ehrenberg, even had his own son burned.

the inquisition

The religious upheaval of the Reformation and Counter-Reformation in Europe also seemed to provoke a period of excessive violence against accused witches. These waves of persecution took place in Protestant as well as Catholic lands and seem to have provided some convenient scapegoats for a populace shocked and bewildered by the rapid changes occurring in their world. The Catholic Church, shaken by the loss of those souls and properties in Protestant countries, became more entrenched and intransigent in its doctrines, prosecuting those, like Galileo, whose theories contradicted the wisdom of the papacy.

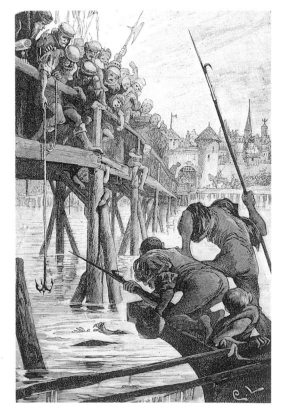

Witches and heretics, both enemies of what was seen as true Christianity, were subject to the ire of the feared Inquisition.

the 1604 statute

In England, witches were hanged rather than burned. Torture took the form of "walking" a witch; that is, securing a confession by sleep deprivation, or "swimming" or "dunking" the accused, who would sink and drown if she were innocent or float if guilty. Water was considered to be a pure element, and it would refuse to swallow up and receive anything that was evil. There were several outbreaks of hysteria regarding witchcraft in England between 1500 and 1700, and again, anything up to 90 percent of the victims were women. The majority of the men accused were directly related to, or in a relationship with, an accused woman. The 1563 statute, made during the reign of Elizabeth I, was more severe than any previous legislation and made it an offense to

witches and heretics, both enemies of what was seen as true christianity, were subject to the ire of the feared inquisition

conjure up spirits even if the intention was good. It had to be proven, however, that witchcraft had caused death in order to invoke the death penalty, and there were lesser penalties within the law for offenses such as employing magic to induce love. It was under James I in 1604 that the law changed, taking account of some of the developments on the continent, including the idea of the diabolical compact. Punishment for a first offense, if evil intent were proven, was now hanging. It was under the new statute of 1604 that the most notorious trials in England occurred.

trial of the lancashire witches

One of the most famous of the English trials is that of the so-called Lancashire witches in 1612. It centered around two families, those of Old Chattox and Old Demdyke, residents of Pendle, each being so poor that they were forced to live by begging and the sale of charms. Old Demdyke, described at the trial as the "rankest hag that ever troubled daylight," had a reputation as a healer. Imputed with the ability to heal, she was also feared as someone who could curse. She allegedly schooled her daughter, Elizabeth Device, and granddaughter, Alizon Device, in witchcraft, and each had a reputation for bewitching people who offended them. Old Chattox had a similar reputation for witchcraft and like Old Demdyke, headed an unpopular family. Old Demdyke's granddaughter was accused of witchcraft, after someone she had reputedly cursed suffered a stroke. She accepted the blame, and was persuaded to implicate her grandmother and Old Chattox, which she did in an attempt to escape punishment. Unfortunately, as a result, eleven family members were hauled to the local Court at Lancaster, and there proceeded the largest witch trial seen in England to that date. Old Chattox and Old Demdyke, both apparently suffering from senile dementia, admitted to trafficking with demons who took the shape of animal familiars, in particular a black cat or a brown dog. Old Demdyke admitted to having sold her soul to a "spirit of devil," calling himself "Tibb." Following the initial arrests, friends and family met in order to hatch an escape plot for those imprisoned in Lancaster castle. However, many of those who attended this escape committee meeting were also accused of witchcraft. One unusual aspect of this case is that it involved a member of one of the wealthier landowning families in the vicinity: Alice Nutter. Although there was no concrete evidence against her, several members of her family and the magistrate who sent Alice to trial stood to profit by her death. The case ended with ten people being hanged at Lancaster and one at York. Five members of Chattox's and Demdyke's families went to the scaffold.

The so-called Lancashire witches gathering to do magic and watched by their sinister familiars.

matthew hopkins—the witchfinder

In Essex, the self-styled witchfinder Matthew Hopkins was responsible for the torment and deaths of numerous alleged witches. At the height of the English Civil War, when the world was, according to some observers, being "turned upside down," it was easy to provide scapegoats for the ills of the country. The widely held belief that there was a Great Chain of Being, a hierarchy of existence in which the king was ordained by God to rule over nobles and commoners, and in which all was in its sanctioned and God-given place, was being torn asunder as parliament waged war against the monarchy. In this time of upheaval, superstition and watching for portents were particularly popular. The suggestion of witches was, by and large, readily accepted by a population that was struggling to come to terms with the upheaval around them and within their very communities. In 1645, aged just twenty-four, Matthew Hopkins accused a number of women in the Manningtree area of Essex of being part of a coven of witches. Essex was already a county associated with witchcraft, following the persecutions of the late 1500s, and his stories of witchcraft were readily accepted. A total of nineteen women were hanged as a result of these accusations. Hopkins' favorite victims were elderly, confused women who lived on the outskirts of society and were disliked by their neighbors. He charged a good deal of money for his investigations, and made a fortune within a short space of time. Hopkins managed to whip up such hysteria that in some cases accusations of causing deaths by bewitchment or the sinking of ships were not even verified by checking that deaths had in fact been caused, or ships sunk. His brief reign as Witchfinder General allowed him to wreak havoc in the neighboring counties of Bedfordshire, Cambridgeshire, Huntingdonshire, and Northamptonshire. However, he finally encountered protests by churchmen and magistrates and, eventually, accusations of witchcraft were leveled against him. Within little over a year, his stint as a witch expert had ended in death for around 200 people, mostly female.

salem

Unexplained deaths or strange illnesses in a neighborhood could be explained by supernatural causes and thus spark a hunt for the agent or witch. In 1692, in Salem, Massachusetts, 165 people, mostly women, were accused of witchcraft and 20 were put to death. This tragedy came about when eight girls and young women between eleven and twenty years of age exhibited strange symptoms of bodily contortions, fits, and writhing. The local physician was unable to account for these fits with any medical explanation, and concluded that the bizarre symptoms must be the result of witchcraft. When questioned, the girls identified a number of women who they readily conceded were the witches responsible for bewitching them. A black slave woman, Tituba, was accused, alongside a number of other women in the white settler community. What was remarkable about the trial was the insistence of the girls that the women were abusing and hurting them from where they stood in the courtroom by sending spectral forms of themselves that no one else could see. The girls then provided dramatic displays of fits, and continued to accuse others from in and around Salem village. Eventually, the local Justice refused to sign any more arrest warrants. He, too, then became accused of witchcraft and had to flee for his life. Despite the efforts of a few local people to try to bring some rationality to bear, the court was swayed by the remarkable symptoms displayed by the girls, and arrests continued. Historians now believe that some of the accusations were based on quarrels between the villagers and farmers in surrounding areas over property

boundaries and land ownership. There is also the suspicion that the symptoms displayed by the girls were consistent with that of an outbreak of ergot poisoning, which produced LSD-type hallucinations and painful body contortions. By 1696 the tide of opinion had turned, partly because of retractions by the original accusers, and partly because the list of the accused had stretched to the family of the Governor of New England. On January 15th, 1697, a display of remorse for having convicted innocent people took place on a day of fasting declared throughout New England.

The hysteria in Salem resulted in the deaths of innocent people. This scene from **The Crucible** *depicts a gathering of witches, so feared by the populace.*

One of those executed at Salem, Alice Lake, was convicted in spite of her denials of ever practicing witchcraft. What she did confess to, however, was becoming pregnant before marriage and attempting, albeit unsuccessfully, to terminate her pregnancy. Having a sexual history and admitting to attempting a self-abortion was enough to convict her of witchcraft, and she was executed. At a time when women's sexuality was closely surveyed and controlled, and destruction of a potential life was a mortal sin, knowledge about childbirth and contraception could result in convictions for witchcraft and child murder. The advent of the professional male medic caused the traditional female midwives to be reviled and pushed into the margins of society where they remained, susceptible to accusations of witchcraft because of their anatomical and herbal knowledge. Such knowledge was the deciding factor in cases of alleged witchcraft in New England, Germany, France, and Italy.

witches in fairy tales

The history of witchcraft is marked by continuity and change. The coming of changes such as the Enlightenment contributed to the witch-hunts diminishing, but persecution of witches did continue into the 19th century in some places, although they were infrequent. Once feared as agents of the Devil, witches now became figures to threaten naughty children with, and they occupied a new space in the popular imagination: the fairy tale.

fairies and witches

It is not surprising that witches ended up in fairy tales, as historically, there have been close cultural links drawn between fairies and witches. Fairy beliefs throughout the world differ in many aspects, but what they all have in common is a connection with the supernatural, and a conviction that fairies, like witches, are different from ordinary human beings. Significantly, fairy lore often overlaps with that of witchcraft, producing superstitions associated with both. The fear of iron, for example, was attributed to both fairies and witches in Europe, as was causing mischief or humans to die or be spirited

fairy beliefs throughout the world differ in many aspects, but what they all have in common is a connection with the supernatural, and a conviction that fairies, like witches, are different from ordinary human beings

away. Fairies and witches were considered not only to be magical beings, but also to be adept at using magic. In some places, the fairies were considered, like witches, to be downright evil. One Christian-based legend has it that when God dropped in on Eve to see how her children were, and to bless them, she had washed only half of them. The other half she hid from God and without God's blessing, they became mischievous and malevolent; these godless creatures were believed to be the fairies.

stealing children

Fairies, like witches, were also blamed for stealing away newborn children. In the case of fairies, the stolen child would be replaced with one of their own race, who would then be brought up by human parents. In the case of witches, the babies were allegedly killed by the witch midwife, to be used as an ingredient in one of the depraved brews they were said to concoct in order to visit evil upon good Christian souls. The threat from fairies and witches toward children is significant in relation to the continuation of the medieval and early modern witchcraft accusations, and to the role of witches in later fairy tales. The evolution of the fairy tale in Europe and the United States during the 19th century produced a number of tales in which children were the main characters. The children were typically in danger from a woman who is attributed with magical powers, and often one who replaces their biological mother following her death. In the tales, the "wicked" stepmother is not always named as a witch, but she has enough in common with the hated witch archetype to make her an honorary one. The stepmother occupies an important place in fairy tales and has much in common with the myth of the evil witch, promoting the witch-hunts of earlier times.

supernatural folktales

Fairy tales are, by and large, folktales containing an element of the supernatural. Many have their origins in oral cultures that prized the ability of storytellers to remember and relate to communities tales of wonder for entertainment and education. Following the growth of literacy, some of these tales were recorded for posterity, but they were altered in the process, to suit the times in which they were written down.

the brothers grimm

In the 19th century, the brothers Grimm set about collecting fairy tales from the oral tradition in Germany, and rewrote them to suit puritanical Protestant sensibilities. The Grimms' versions of the traditional fairy tales were highly moralistic, and depicted a world in which good boys and girls were defined by their long-suffering and industrious characters. Bad boys and girls, on the other hand, were lazy and disobedient, and were severely punished. The most popular of their tales were rewritten by various European publishers, and were extensively altered versions of the stories by the time they reached Victorian England. The "taming" process started by the Grimms was applied, in turn, to the European publisher's stories, and subsequent altered versions of the tales, so that by the 20th century they had become stories especially for children.

The nursery versions of the fairy tales are now so familiar that most parents of small children can relate at least some of the most popular stories without recourse to a book. Most of these famous tales contain references to a "wicked" witch, or at least an evil female figure with many of the characteristics usually attributed to witches.

the wicked stepmother

One of the most famous child abusers in popular fairy tales is the witch in *Hansel and Gretel*. In some versions of the tale, the witch's true identity is revealed to be that of the children's evil stepmother. The story centers around the abandoning of the children in the woods. Hansel and Gretel's stepmother persuades their father that they are too poor to maintain his son and daughter. In some versions, the poor woodcutter father agrees to lead the children into the woods and "lose" them. However, the first couple of attempts to do this end in failure because Hansel, who has overheard the plot, lays a trail of white pebbles to guide them back out of

> **one of the most famous child abusers in popular fairy tales is the witch in *hansel and gretel*. In some versions of the tale, the witch's true identity is revealed to be that of the...evil stepmother**

the forest. The third time, their stepmother, who has discovered this ruse, prevents Hansel from taking stones in his pockets and the children are forced to use their last piece of bread to lay the trail. However, birds eat the bread and the children are left stranded. After a while they come to a gingerbread house, which they begin to eat. The evil witch who owns this house captures them, forces Gretel to be housekeeper, and incarcerates Hansel in a cage to be eaten at a future date. However, the witch is near-sighted and Hansel is able to fool her by presenting her each day with a stick, instead of his finger, which she tests daily in order to gauge his body fat. Eventually, the witch loses patience with Hansel's inability to gain weight and orders Gretel to prepare a hot oven for her brother. Gretel cleverly persuades the witch to crawl into the oven to see if it is hot enough, and shuts her in to die horribly, while she helps her brother escape. In some versions of the tale, the children are guided home, with the help of either their dead mother or a magical bird, only to find their stepmother has gone and their repentant father joyfully welcomes them back.

beyond temptation

Analysis of this tale highlights intriguing similarities between older witchcraft beliefs and the new place occupied by the witch of the tale. For example, if we take it that the evil stepmother is really an aspect of the witch in the forest, we see that she can exercise sexual allure over the father, who then errs from protecting his children. This fits the image of the oversexed female, easily given to evil, as depicted some 500 years before in the *Malleus Malificarum* and in numerous trials afterwards throughout Europe and the United States. That she is a threat to children, to the point of cannibalism, is a direct reference to the tales told of witches' Sabbats, and the baby fat allegedly used as an ingredient in the flying ointment with which the witches were said to fly to meet the Devil. The good characters in the tale are the dead mother, the clever and resourceful children, and, oddly enough, their father. The new stepmother and the evil witch represent all that is bad about women, but the biological mother is "safe" as a good character because she is dead, and thus beyond temptation by her "naturally" bad character. The father is exonerated because he has been led astray by an evil woman—a witch—echoing much older fears that witches can disempower and ensnare men. In fairy tales, the good mother is represented by the ever-faithful dead woman, and the bad mother is represented by the witch.

rapunzel

The story of *Snow White* exemplifies many of the witch characteristics described here. Similarly, the tales of *Rapunzel* and *Sleeping Beauty* also contain evil witches who imprison adolescent girls in order to keep them from men, thereby using magic to frustrate male desire. More modern forms of the fairy tale have continued to vilify witches, and by extension, women who do not conform to orthodox femininity, in ways that would not have seemed out of place during the witchcraft persecutions of the 15th to 18th centuries.

Hansel and Gretel meet the wicked witch outside her home. In some versions of the tale, the witch turns out to be their stepmother.

the present day

Over the last 30 years or so, efforts have been made to subvert the form of the fairy tale in order to give children a more positive view of the people most affected by the archetypes in them. Over time, some of these archetypes have become oppressive stereotypes. Modern versions of Grimm's fairy tales have been attacked by feminists for instilling passive representations of girls and highly negative images of older women, in particular, as witches.

A number of new versions of fairy tales now exist, including some alternative and rewritten versions of older ones, including M.M. Kaye's *The Ordinary Princess*, and the feminist collection of tales entitled *Don't Bet on the Prince*. Angela Carter's famously dark reworkings of familiar fairy tales and the Clarissa Pinkola Estes book, *Women Who Run with the Wolves*, have become modern classics of this revisionist genre. However, the archetypes of the older fairy tales still have a great deal of power, as does the continued use of negative images of witches in modern renditions of them.

hollywood witches

Walt Disney's first full-length cartoon feature of 1937, *Snow White*, featured a witch who represented a truly terrifying version of the evil stepmother archetype. The murderous stepmother portrayed in the film is endowed with magical powers, including the ability to transform herself into a hag who gives the eponymous heroine a poisoned apple. The image of the evil Queen shrieking, enraged, before the mirror that declared Snow White the fairest of them all, haunted young audiences through the generations.

In 1959, Disney produced a film called *Sleeping Beauty*. This time, the Sleeping Beauty has a wicked fairy, named Malificent, a name reminiscent of the crime of which most witches in "The Burning Times" were accused: *maleficia* (ill-doing). She is a fearsome character who not only condemns Princess Aurora to die on her 16th birthday, but changes into a fire-breathing dragon, whose efforts to kill the prince provided young audiences with the spectacle of the prince threatened by the monstrous witch.

hocus pocus

The Disney film of recent times that most promoted the figure of evil witches was the 1993 hit *Hocus Pocus*, starring Bette Midler, Kathy Najimi, and Sarah Jessica Parker. A direct reference is made to the Salem witch-hunts by setting the story in Salem, Massachussetts. Early in the film, there is a distasteful scene that shows the witches killing a child in order to cast a spell to retain their youth and beauty. When the witches

The 1998 romantic film
Practical Magic,
starring Sandra Bullock
and Nicole Kidman,
continued the myth that
witchcraft is an
inherited trait.

are inadvertently brought back to life by a group of youngsters on Halloween, the youngest witch flies through the sky over Salem attempting to draw children towards them for a repeat of the spell that will make them youthful again. At the time, many pagans were dismayed by the implications of the film, which directly appealed to the old prejudice that witches stole away and sacrificed children. Those familiar with the history of Salem were outraged that the innocent victims of the 17th-century witch-hunt were once again being portrayed as evil. Significantly, the pagan community was being accused of the "Satanic Abuse" of children at this time by fundamentalist groups in the United States and elsewhere. This myth was eventually laid to rest after it was found that the rumors were unfounded. However, *Hocus Pocus* played up to these prejudices and showed extreme insensitivity to witches and the memory of those killed at Salem.

female misfits

The Craft, a modern parable of magic and the nature of power, came to the screens in 1996. Here, the protagonists are an all-female group of misfits who discover that they can gain access to magical powers. It is a teenage movie with a hip soundtrack and a cast of young actors who became fashion and attitude role models for girls and young

women everywhere. The script is one of teenage angst and rebellion, flavored with magical powers and the lessons of responsibility. Guided by a Wiccan advisor, the film is a far more responsible portrayal of the nature of witchcraft and power than any produced in mainstream cinema to date. However, the witchcraft presented in *The Craft* owes more to flashy special effects, post-feminist angst, and the expectations of Hollywood than it does to the reality of the Craft itself. Pagans were split on whether it was a positive or negative representation of the Craft, most agreeing that it both sensationalized and trivialized what is, for all of us a spiritual and responsible path.

positive media witches

Not all popular cultural portrayals of witches are as mixed, or as negative, as those found in

The ugliness and evil attributed to witches is encompassed in the terrifying Wicked Witch of the West from the 1939 film, **The Wizard of Oz.**

mainstream cinema. Television shows in particular have for the last few years begun to present genuinely popular characters such as *Sabrina the Teenage Witch*. Although Sabrina inherits her witchcraft, and gets into a number of scrapes through the misuse of somewhat showy spells, she is a generally sympathetic character, echoing her housewife ancestor Samantha, of the 1960s television hit, *Bewitched*. An equally popular teen character is found in *Buffy the Vampire Slayer*, another character who, like Sabrina, inherits her admittedly bloodthirsty characteristics and employs them in the eternal battle of good against evil. The show includes the character Willow, a friend of Buffy, who is a witch. Her gentle, ethical approach to magic appears to be a genuine attempt to take into account contemporary ideas around witchcraft, and the character is popular with the show's audience. The Sabrina and Willow characters may mirror the popular misunderstanding of magical powers being inherited, but they are positive interpretations in what has been a largely hostile environment for witches: the media of television and film.

Charmed, like *Sabrina* and *Buffy the Vampire Slayer*, also relies on the premise that magical powers are inherited, and uses special effects to enable witches to make objects fly across the room and time stand still. However, this show more than any other attempts to portray witches in a positive light. Although the series has provided plenty of amusement for contemporary witches because of its mistakes and regular misrepresentations of contemporary Craft customs, most witches agree that in terms of public relations, it has at best been slightly more positive than usual, and at worst, simply harmless.

fantasy literature

Contemporary interest in magic and mythology has provided writers, filmmakers, and television companies with a range of new material. The public's ongoing interest in all things magical has generated a number of television shows, such as *Robin Hood*, *Xena: Warrior Princess*, and *Hercules: the Legendary Journeys*, all of which contain positive and negative portrayals of pagan gods and goddesses, sorcerers, magicians, and witches. In the late 20th and early 21st century, fantasy fiction has provided the most positive portrayals of paganism, in particular Marion Zimmer Bradley's rewriting of the Arthurian Legends in *Mists of Avalon*. Fantasy literature abounds with positive images of magic, magicians, and witches. The British children's writer Alan Garner has rewritten Welsh and Cheshire legends and folklore in his range of novels on magic, the most notable of which is *The Owl Service*. Tamara Pierce's *Lyonesse* books, which are fantasy novels for young readers, are based on a positive teenage heroine, Alanna, who is unself-consciously feminist, assertive, and at home with magic. More recently, J K Rowling has enthralled adults and youngsters alike with tales of enchantment in her *Harry Potter* series of books.

Not all portrayals of witches are as evil man- and child-ensnaring harridans. However, the figure of the evil witch still has a certain amount of cultural currency in the 21st century, and popular culture continues, occasionally, to cash in on it. This figure has its origins not in the mysterious mists of time, or in the primeval fears of humankind, but specifically in the climate of hatred and fear generated during the witchcraft persecutions of the medieval and early modern periods. The witch continues to be an ambiguous figure in the modern imagination, capable of curing or cursing. The truth, as ever, lies waiting for those who genuinely want to know what witchcraft is about, and who are ready to let witches tell their own stories.

oday's witchcraft is a world away from the myth of the malevolent hag or the modern myth of the Devil-worshipping housewife. Its reality is also removed from more benevolent though equally inaccurate media portrayals of a "super-babe" with amazing hereditary powers. This chapter will introduce you to the different types of witchcraft, explore what it means to be a witch in the 21st century, and explain how to become a witch.

Present-day witchcraft is a thriving and growing spiritual path, and modern-day witches are found all over the globe. All of our practices are inevitably flavored by our cultures, our politics, our history, and our different interests. While some of us prefer our own background culture or heritage as the basis for our type of witchcraft—for example, Celtic or African—others are inspired by a mixture of cultural backgrounds. Some witches follow a strictly defined framework of graduation through different levels of their chosen tradition, while others prize a more informal arrangement. Some witches work in groups or covens and others prefer to work alone. Such diversity and flexibility are considered to be a positive part of the richness and strength of the Craft.

Witches who live in parts of Europe, the United States, and Australasia can work openly in communities, hold public rituals to celebrate the eight festivals, and become involved in environmental campaigns. Those of us who live in reasonably tolerant circumstances can be open about who and what we are, and we value this freedom highly. However, in some places, especially Africa and South America, practicing magic is punished severely by law, and the risk of discovery has driven some traditions underground. In most places in the West, witchcraft is making a comeback, due to a general interest in "alternative spiritualities" and the increased confidence with which we identify ourselves and practice our beliefs.

different paths

There are many different paths that come under the heading of "witchcraft" or "the Craft," just as witchcraft is only one spiritual path that comes under the heading of "paganism." These embody a variety of preferences and approaches, all of which add up to a diverse mixture of spiritual and magical paths that encompass "Witchcraft."

wicca

The first type of witchcraft to emerge from the 1950s revival became known as "Wicca"—purportedly coming from the Anglo-Saxon word for "wise." The masculine of this word is "Wicca," the feminine is "Wicce," meaning "wise ones." Some commentators have disputed the origin of these words, and the word "witch," implying that they actually mean "bendy." However, the latter description is still quite fitting, as witches continually work with flow and change, so flexibility is a good attribute to have.

Initially, Wicca evolved in Britain from two main schools, known as Gardnerian and Alexandrian Wicca. The first is the path described by Gerald Gardner, the second a development of Gardner's system by Alex and Maxine Sanders. Both systems are coven-based and have a structure of initiation and a degree system through which the initiates are trained before graduating. Most Wiccan covens in Britain and the United States are mixtures of these different traditions, and have evolved customs and structures of their own. In the United States, many types of witchcraft are described as "Wicca," in Britain, "Wicca" refers to a particular type. This type of witchcraft is still largely coven-based, although not as stringent about numbers as once stipulated. The old belief about thirteen witches in a coven reflects the optimum number that could make a coven operational and manageable. It is a number prized in witchcraft, as the number of moon cycles in a year, but having thirteen in a coven is not a strict rule.

hereditaries

Witchcraft encompasses a number of traditions that have evolved over the last forty years. One type of witchcraft that claims to be much older than the 20th-century revival is that of the "Hereditary" witch, or the witch who has had Craft knowledge passed down through his or her family. Hereditaries often claim to have an unbroken line of knowledge passed from, usually, mother to daughter for many thousands of years. This is regarded with some scepticism by most non-Hereditary witches. However, as Hereditaries generally keep to themselves, there is little debate in witchcraft circles other than about the origins of their Craft knowledge.

solitaries

Another increasingly common type of witch is the individual who practices mostly alone, is self-taught, and occasionally joins with other witches and pagans to celebrate the festivals. This is the "Hedge Witch," so called because of the association between lone witches and the tradition of the village wise woman or cunning man. These people were expected to have a great deal of herbal and magical or "cunning" knowledge. The herbs and plants they used, and the nature spirits with whom they reputedly communed, were thought to be found in or under hedgerows; so the term "Hedge Witch" was coined. "Hedge Witches," or healers, could use the plant in a hedge for healing or could also disappear into a hedge if necessary. Today the expression refers to solo workers, some of whom prefer to call themselves "Solitaries," or variations on

solo workers generally conduct esbats and spell-casting alone, and occasionally share circle space with others for seasonal celebrations

"Hedge Witch" such as "Kitchen Witch" or "Ditch Witch," or simply "Witch." Solo workers generally conduct Esbats and spell-casting alone, and occasionally share circle space with others for seasonal celebrations. However, there is a growing movement toward such witches uniting with others for different purposes, including full-moon celebrations and magic. Many of these witches still class themselves as Solitaries because they do not owe allegiance to any type of coven or group, despite finding themselves working more often with other people than alone.

gay and feminist witchcraft

There are many different types of witchcraft originating from the 1960s and 1970s, a number of which emerged from the women's and the gay movement. Groups of people were interested in witchcraft but found some of its principles unable to accommodate their politics or sexual orientation. They therefore created new paths for themselves during this time. One of the problems these groups encountered was the strict adherence of many Wiccan groups to sexual bipolarity, derived from Jungian psychology. This holds that all men and women have a contrasexual side: women have a "masculine" side, or animus, and men have a "feminine" side, or anima. The insistence

Diana, the hunter goddess, kept away from men and is the ideal deity for those witches wanting to work in an environment free from the presence of men.

of some covens that this was an immovable fact was off-putting for many who found this sexist and antigay in practice. Feminists, lesbians, and gay men formed their own groups, which were more progressive and inclusive, and so created a number of new paths in witchcraft. One of them is known as "Dianic Wicca," a women-only tradition. Dianic groups were originally lesbian, but some now include heterosexual women. The name "Dianic" refers to the goddess Diana, who kept separate from men. She is an obvious reference point for lesbians, heterosexual women, and feminists wishing to celebrate their spirituality in a women-only space. Dianic witchcraft is not about rejecting men but reclaiming female space in a patriarchal world. The women who celebrate together in this space find it empowering to be with other women. Similarly, the Radical Faerie tradition, which is predominantly male and gay, claims separate space for gay and bisexual men, and sometimes lesbian or bisexual women.

global deities and cultures

Other paths have been created through a predominant interest in particular flavors of paganism. Some witches are drawn to Egyptian deities, for example, whereas others are drawn to the Celtic traditions. Traditional Gardnerian and Alexandrian Wicca honors a number of deities from different world traditions and mythologies. However, for those who are attracted to a particular group of traditions, deities, or culture, celebrating in accordance with that tradition is naturally more satisfying. Usually, someone takes an interest in a particular culture or mythology and develops a system of witchcraft from it. This can take years of study, meditation, and ritual in order to produce a workable system in which they can celebrate with other like-minded people. Those witches who arrive after a new path is created have the advantages of being able to celebrate in a way that is suited to them, and of molding the tradition as it continues to evolve.

The Norse Tradition is a brand of witchcraft based on Nordic mythology and culture that honors the Nordic gods and goddesses including Odin, Freya, Thor, and Loki. This tradition draws upon Norse mythology, literature, and customs to celebrate the cycle of the year, to work ritual, and to divine the future through the ancient system of the runes. There is also a Saxon tradition of witchcraft, which has a following in Britain and in the United States. This draws upon Saxon culture, deities, and traditions. For those drawn to the Greek gods and goddesses that came to us from the Hellenic period in Greece, there is already a body of literature and a pantheon of gods and goddesses upon which to draw for inspiration. Those witches who are drawn to the Egyptian deities tend also to attempt to

witchcraft is a rainbow path; multicolored and changing, shifting, improving, and growing

recreate ancient rituals as described in writings found in the pyramids and on archaeological digs. As some groups prefer to draw upon a tradition that has a large body of extant literature, it is relatively easy to construct a system of ritual and magic from them.

witchcraft for the individual

The witchcraft described in this book would be recognized by most of these traditions as authentic witchcraft. There will always be those who claim that only traditional Gardnerian or Alexandrian Wicca is true witchcraft, just as there will always be those who claim that self-initiation is not a true initiation. These people need to be reminded of the history of the tradition that they are claiming is the only "true" one. Wicca did not emerge until the 1950s in Britain, in spite of its original claims to have been passed down unaltered through generations from ancient times. Even since the 1950s, many aspects of it have been changed to accommodate new understandings. Witchcraft was never formulated as a hierarchical degree system, nor as a group organization. If you decide to join the Craft, take courage in the fact that witchcraft is a rainbow path, multicolored and changing, shifting, improving, and growing.

All witches have in common their pagan spirituality, their reverence for the goddess in whatever form they perceive her, the practice of magic, and the code of ethics that holds that we must "harm none." Even witches within traditional covens have to develop their own spiritual path, one that is meaningful to the individual. Witchcraft is a path that has to be defined by the individual for the individual. Anything less is not in the spirit of witchcraft.

becoming a witch

Becoming a witch is not difficult. You are deciding to embrace a life-enhancing and joyful spiritual path. You are declaring that you are willing to experience the wonders of the magical web and encounter the gods and/or goddesses. You are daring to be different in a way that facilitates your growth and empowers you. You are choosing to encounter spirit without the mediation of doctrine or orthodoxy. Most important, you are stepping into the spiral dance of life, celebrated by witches all over the world.

valuing yourself

What is required in order to call yourself "witch" with integrity and pride is that you practice the ethical tenets of the Wiccan Rede. Study your own history as a witch, find those traditions that hold meaning for you, connect with the magical web, and find the goddess within and around you. In addition, you need to learn how to work ritual and magic, methods of raising, containing, and releasing power, how to work with the energies of sun, moon, and earth, and the principles of sympathetic magic upon which

study your own history as a witch, find those traditions that hold meaning for you, connect with the magical web, and find the goddess within and around you

most witchcraft magic is based. You will learn to work with intuition alongside rationality, explore your dreams and desires, and determine who you really are. Becoming a witch means valuing yourself as a unique being. This is a difficult task if you have been brought up to believe that self-denial and diffidence equal goodness.

growth and awareness

Witches are frequently asked, after they have explained all of the above, "Yes, but how do you actually become a witch?" The expectation that there must be a particular method or moment at which you change into a witch probably comes from popular ideas about the nature of witchcraft and magic. Some people who become interested in witchcraft also have expectations that witches are gifted with amazing powers as the result of a particular ceremony or spell. The truth is more mundane than the fantasy. Witchcraft is about growing your own spirituality, making contact with the web of magic, learning how to weave, and observing the way that the world works. It is often assumed that witches can move things around at will or change events and outcomes through spellwork. In reality, witchcraft is about working with natural energies, observing how they work, and determining how you can gently divert them. At the same time, such actions change us, too. Witches do not stand outside the great web of existence; on the contrary, they consciously become more a part of it. Growth and awareness, therefore, are the key elements in becoming a witch.

The decision to become a witch is not one you should take lightly. It is not a persona you can put on or take off. It permeates your whole life, and can drastically change your perception of the world. Becoming a witch will affect everything and everyone around you. That it will affect them positively doesn't alter the fact that you will relate to them differently, and you should be prepared for this.

inner magic

To become a witch is to become changed within yourself and a changer of things outside you. This is your inner magic. Encountering the goddess, working with magic, and connecting with nature will take a lot of time and energy until it becomes second nature to you. You may find that you get annoyed with those people who do not understand witchcraft or paint it as "evil," but you will have to resist putting them right until you have grasped some of the key concepts for yourself. This can be achieved only through experience, and this means practicing patience.

others' perceptions

Once you choose to tell your friends and family about your new spiritual path, you may also find yourself being cast as an all-knowing wise one who can solve all the world's ills with magic. Handling this attitude from friends and family takes confidence in your own knowledge and abilities, and again this is something that comes with experience. Other people's ideas of what a witch is, or should be, can be a great burden if you are not yet confident in this identity. People who are secure in their self-identity feel less threatened by such ideas. If you are secure in yourself, you feel strong and you can develop the ability to be gentle with those who may mean well but have odd ideas. The ability to be tolerant and

you may be inundated with requests for healing, love spells, and curses and consulted over personal or health problems

understanding of the misconceptions of others is much more in keeping with the ethic that teaches us to harm none. Although we have a right to stand up for ourselves, we do have to consider that not everyone is as well informed in witchcraft, and they may struggle to come to terms with it. One way in which well-meaning people attempt to identify witches positively is to say, "Oh, so you're a white witch." The implication of this reaction is that witchcraft is generally evil but there are a few good ones. At this point, you will have to choose whether to tell them bluntly that they've got it wrong, or smile and explain that witchcraft doesn't work like that and as you work toward helping the environment, you prefer to be known as a green witch. The former reaction risks alienating people who probably mean well, whereas the second doesn't cost too much in time and energy and will help shift their understanding along a little in a good-humored way.

superpowers

Another reason for being careful about what to reveal to whom, and in which way, is the tendency for people to believe you are endowed with superpowers because you have announced that you are a witch. You may be inundated with requests for healing, love spells, and curses and consulted over personal or health problems into which you have no more insight than you did before. This sort of reaction is much better in many ways than the sort of response that declares you to be dangerous or mad, but it does bring problems of its own. When people's often unreasonable expectations are disappointed, you are just as suddenly declared to be a charlatan or a fake. Take care about who you tell and what you say until you are confident enough for these possible reactions not to matter to you.

lady in black

It is tempting, once you have decided that witchcraft is for you, to adopt a new outward persona, and there are lots of attractive, witchy personas for new witches to imitate. There is the siren, sexy, alluring, and irresistible. There is Morgan Le Fey, gothic, mysterious, and rather shady, and there is Medea, forbidding and vengeful. Playing with a new persona can be a lot of fun, particularly if it involves assembling a new wardrobe. This new wardrobe may be mostly black and purple, and you may choose to deck yourself out with pentacle earrings, rings, and pendants. You may also favor wearing lots of eyeliner. However, you should remember that this is just playing and it doesn't make anyone more of a witch than if they are simply wearing jeans and sneakers. One of the great dangers in dressing up like this is that you may find yourself conforming to other people's stereotypes. The witch clad in black is an age-old image. Although for witches black is the color of deep creativity, the inner self, and the mysteries of the universe, it may be seen by others as negative, evil, or affected. "Dressing the part" is very tempting, but it can also turn out to be humiliating in the long run.

although for witches black is the color of deep creativity, the inner self, and the mysteries of the universe, it may be seen by others as negative, evil, or affected

individual path

Once your decision is made, you have already stepped onto the path of witchcraft. The next step depends on the type of person you are. If you are a fiery, adventurous sort of person, you will probably wish to throw yourself into studying everything at once. If you are more cautious or laid back, you may wish to learn gradually and thoroughly. One of the lessons that the Craft teaches is to be resourceful; this means doing what makes sense in the context of your own life.

The information, guidance, exercises, and rituals in this book will help you on your path. None of these assume that you are going to go through an initiation ritual, or that you are taking a particular traditional path. Witchcraft is about mixing and matching, to find what suits best. You should treat this book as a smorgasbord of information and guidance, to be selected and chosen according to taste.

initiation

To be initiated into witchcraft is to be introduced to spirit as a witch and to offer, in turn, an undertaking that you are committed to the Craft's ethics and principles. Spiritual initiations in different cultures involve a number of common features, which usually include being formally introduced to the spirits or gods, taking an oath, having a visionary experience, and receiving wisdom. An initiation into the Craft is a rite of passage that declares your readiness to enter into the realm of the circle and your preparedness to learn from what you find there. This is a serious undertaking, but not a solemn one, as witchcraft is joyful and celebratory. Initiation into the Craft, therefore, is a happy occasion, even if it is marked by serious words.

formal recognition

In the Craft, initiation is regarded in two different ways. One view is that it is simply a formalization of one's decision to become a witch. When a person recognizes, accepts, or decides that they want to be a witch, they have usually been going down that path for some time. Most witches at initiation could look back and say that there

an initiation into the craft is a rite of passage that declares your readiness to enter into the realm of the circle and your preparedness to learn from what you find there

wasn't really a moment when they became a witch, they were already further along the path than they thought. What they see in retrospect is that the journey toward this moment was gradual. The point at which they acknowledge that they want to be a witch and decide to become initiated is usually some time after they have actually started to be one. Accordingly, initiation is seen by some as a ritual that marks your growth as a witch, your preparedness to be known by that name, and your acceptance by others into the community of the Craft.

catalyst for change

The other way of viewing initiation is that it is a catalyst that invokes rather than simply recognizes one's status as a witch. This version of initiation considers the ritual as the time when we are drawing attention to ourselves at a cosmic level, alerting and inviting spirit to change us in some way. Our declaration that we are witches and priest/esses is seen as more than a formality, it is making contact with the goddess, elements, and the great web of being, and introducing ourselves as priest/ess, witch, and weaver. In return, the goddess, element, and web empower us, send us visions,

at initiation, we actively step over the threshold between our old life and our new life as a witch

and shape us into the witches we wish to be. It has often been observed years later, by witches who have undergone initiation, that the year after initiation was one of the most disruptive and topsy-turvy years of their lives, bringing major life changes. These have involved house moves, changes of career, the ending of outgrown relationships and the creation of new relationships, and even new babies. This does not mean that initiation will automatically result in all these changes. It is simply an observation on how some lives change after initiation, and an appreciation of how powerful the process can be. At initiation, we actively step over the threshold between our old life and our new life as a witch. At this time, we also invite the goddess to help us change and grow within our lives and as individuals.

patience

Whatever version you decide is the more truer for you, initiation is a powerful experience. You are declaring yourself, your aims, and your affinities to the goddess, the elements, the great web, and to the community of witches past and present. Whether you become self-initiated or are initiated into a group, provided that your intentions are genuine, then your desire is authentic and the changes you wish for will come to you. Be prepared to be patient; sometimes the most effective magic is that which works slowly, sometimes almost imperceptibly. When this happens, change is sometimes noticed a long time after it has started, but it is equally significant.

magical name

One feature of initiation is that you choose a magical name with which to enter this new phase of your life. It is customary to choose the name before the ceremony so that you can declare it when you identify yourself as willing to enter the circle. Another feature is that you receive the tools of the Craft, all of which should be consecrated prior to the ritual (see pp 126–7). Although the tools vary in number and content according to tradition, they usually include an athame (pron: "ath-aye-mee"), or witch's knife, a wand, a pentagram, a chalice, and cords.

cords and measures

The cords are used in the ceremony to measure the candidate's height, circumference of head, and length around the chest and arms—all "shroud" measurements. There is nothing sinister about this: they record our unique vital statistics. These cords, or "measures" as they are known, partly imitate the birth cord by which we were connected to our mothers. In the context of initiation, they connect us with spirit. Most witches believe we are most directly connected with spirit before birth and after death, when we are part of the whole, rather than individuals. At initiation, we pass from one life into another, and the cords symbolize the umbilical cord by which we are connected with spirit again at this time.

A witch's measures are kept very safe, because of the intimate connection between the measures and the witch herself. It was once believed that a person could be harmed if an enemy had access to something very closely connected to them, such as a lock of hair, drop of blood, or item kept in their possession; the measures of a witch fall into this category. In more dangerous times, measures were kept by the coven to ensure secrecy. Today, they are usually handed back to the candidate, to emphasize that the candidate is not under duress as a result of their initiation, and that they are completely free to follow their heart, even if this means choosing to leave the group at some time in the future.

high priestess and priest

People becoming initiated in a group usually have a sponsor, with whom they work and train prior to becoming accepted for initiation. This sponsor may be the High Priestess or Priest, if you work in a more traditional Wiccan group, or someone who is further along the path in terms of experience. The custom of having only males initiating females and vice versa has been challenged recently by more progressive groups and individuals, who believe that the sex of the "initiator" is immaterial, since it is actually the goddess who initiates witches. In more traditional Wicca, there are three different degrees of initiation, the second and third of which are often taken together. The second declares you a "High Priest/ess," and the third entitles you to "hive off" from the mother coven and begin a coven of your own. The third degree involves what is known as the "Great Rite," a ritual that includes a symbolic representation of sexual intercourse using a chalice and athame to represent the male and female, or actual intercourse between a committed couple who are undergoing third-degree initiation together. What should never, ever happen is that your sponsor or teacher demands sex from you in return for initiation. If anyone should suggest this at any point, leave immediately. Persuasion, coercion, and soliciting sexual favors are not in line with any kind of witchcraft ethic, and this sort of behavior is simply abusive. It is extremely rare for this to happen, but unfortunately, there are unscrupulous people who will masquerade as teachers or gurus in order to obtain power and gratification. These people are not witches.

self-initiation

If you are choosing a solo path, or cannot or do not wish to join a group for the present, you will need to be largely self-taught prior to, and following, initiation. Books can be very helpful tools for learning about the history of magic and witchcraft, providing exercises and inspiration for rituals and spells. The information and exercises in this book will help you prepare for initiation. Keeping a dream diary to record all your dreams and any recurrent imagery or symbols will help your preparations, as will starting a Book of Shadows, which lists rituals, spells, results, snippets of wisdom, and

initiation may happen at the beginning of, or further down, your spiritual path. What matters is that you are ready and comfortable that the time is right for you

chants. Meeting other witches at conventions and festivals is also recommended as a way of gaining advice and guidance prior to your initiation.

Initiation may happen at the beginning of, or further down, your spiritual path. What matters is that you are ready and comfortable that the time is right for you. If you choose to join a group, you usually have to wait until your sponsor or the group decide that you are ready for initiation. If a group considers that you are ready before you believe you are, then you should not feel pressured to take such a significant step. Any group worth joining will respect your wishes to wait until the time is right.

initiation rituals

Initiation ceremonies in witchcraft are structured and angled differently in accordance with the tradition into which you are being initiated, and whether you are being initiated in a group or solitary situation. You will sometimes find differences in style, content, and structure across different groups even within the same tradition. Self-initiation is a largely self-assembled affair, so this, too, differs between individuals.

common elements

Despite the differences, initiation ceremonies that take place in groups have some things in common. Most contain all or some of the following elements:

Entering the circle naked.
A challenge on entering the circle.
Questioning to establish whether the candidate truly understands the serious nature of initiation.
The taking of a magical or "witch" name.
A promise to protect one's brothers and sisters in the Craft.
An undertaking never to betray the sacred trust of knowledge delivered to you in the circle.
Vows of dedication to the goddess.
The taking of measures.
The five-fold blessing.
Revelation of Craft or group secrets, names, and lineage.
Introduction to the five elements as witch and priest/priestess.

purity

Nudity is a way of entering the circle in purity, innocence, and honesty. Not all covens insist on nudity, but most make an exception for initiation. Most witches would argue that since we are born naked into this world, we should be similarly unencumbered when we cross the threshold at initiation from our old life into the new.

fear

Sometimes, a candidate is blindfolded and led to the circle, where s/he asks for admission. Whether blindfolded or not, the candidate is challenged, usually at the point of a sword or with his/her way barred by a gatekeeper. The challenger will warn the candidate that it is better that s/he should fall upon the sword, or be barred from entry rather than enter with fear in his/her heart. The challenge does not require you to be without fear, but that being fearful, you proceed anyway. The candidate is further challenged by elected members of the group as to his/her understanding of the seriousness of initiation. This offers the group an opportunity to explain fully and in a formal way, what is expected of the candidates offering themselves for initiation. It is also an opportunity for the candidates to have the responsibilities of the undertaking spelled out to them.

revelations

It is customary for those presenting themselves for initiation to have a magical name prepared. Once the initiatory part of the ceremony is over, and the candidate is declared witch and priest/ess, it is usual for others in the group to reveal their magical names, the secret name of the coven, and its lineage.

taking of the oath

Joining this family of the Craft also entails responsibility toward others within it. A solemn oath, derived from the fears of darker times when discovery meant torment and death, is taken by the candidate. Witches' measures are also taken at this time.

five-fold kiss

To welcome the new witch, many covens perform the "five-fold kiss." In this part of the ritual, the new witch is kissed by the initiator on the places named, which traditionally were feet, knees, womb/phallus, breasts, and mouth. Today, some people prefer the five-fold blessing, by which the new witch is anointed with oil. The newly consecrated witch and priest/priestess is then introduced by their magical name to the elements.

The formal part of the ceremony is usually accompanied by "cakes and ale," or drink and food, or a party in honor of the new group member.

The following ritual is a self-initiation ceremony, designed for those who either have chosen not to join a group, or who wish to become initiated at the present time but do not have access to group membership. It is customary to wait a year and a day between deciding to become initiated and actually doing so. This is a good guide, as it allows you to go through one solar year, taking on board the seasonal festivals, and the different energies and cycles, prior to dedicating yourself to this path. It also gives you a chance to find a magical name and assemble some magical tools, in particular an athame, that you should have for the initiation ritual.

self-initiation ritual

preparation

Prior to initiation, you should read and work through all the exercises in this book. Ask yourself why you wish to become a witch, and see if your answers satisfy you. Consider how you interpret the Wiccan Rede, "An it harm none, do thy will," and how you will put this into action in everyday life.

Ensure complete privacy for this ritual, prepare a space, and light candles all around it. Take a bath in darkness, dry yourself, and enter the candlelit room naked.

you will need

Initiation incense, made from one part frankincense, one part myrrh, and one part juniper berries. A yellow, red, blue, and green candle arranged clockwise around the circle with a purple candle in the center. Your athame, placed at the center of the circle. One tablespoon of olive, grapeseed, or almond oil, with one drop of chamomile oil. A 6–9 ft. (2.5m) length each of green and red cord. The cord should be as tall or taller than the candidate. One glass of red wine or dark juice, and some bread in the center of the room.

the ritual

✶ Cast a circle (see p. 106), light the incense, and welcome the elements, beginning with air, saying respectively:

Watchtower of the east (south/west/north), the element of air (fire/water/earth), I call upon you to witness and guard this circle.

✶ Light the yellow (red/blue/green) candles, after each speech of welcome, saying "Hail and welcome" after each one is lit. Before the purple candle, say:

Hecate, Goddess of Witches and Watcher at the Crossroads, I stand now at a Crossroads between the old life and the new. Bless me, spirit, element of transformation, and carry me on my journey to be a witch and priest/ess of the Goddess.

Light the candle. Stand before the spirit candle, and take deep breaths, counting 100 heartbeats. Say aloud:

I stand on the threshold between my old life and my new, and I am willing to cross over and become witch and priest/ess. I am willing to endure in order to learn, and offer two perfect words as I cross into the unknown: love and trust.

✳ Take your athame and move around the circle clockwise, and, beginning with air, introduce yourself to each element:

Element of air/fire/water/earth/spirit, know me as (your magical name), as witch and priest/ess of the Goddess.

✳ Now that you are back in the center, pause for another 100 heartbeats, then take the oil and anoint your body in this variation of the "five-fold blessing," anointing your center forehead on the last line, not your eyes:

Blessed be my feet that have brought me on this path, blessed be my sex, source of love and power, blessed be my breasts, and the heart that beats within, blessed be my lips that will speak the sacred names, blessed be my eyes that will see clearly the path before me.

✳ Pause for 100 heartbeats, then take the green and red cords and fasten them together at the end. Measure your height, toe to crown, and fasten a knot in the double cord. Measure the circumference of your head with the cord, and fasten another knot at that point. Measure around your chest and arms at heart level, and fasten a knot at this point. These are your measures and should be kept safe. Then say aloud:

I promise to protect my brothers and sisters in the Craft and never betray the sacred trust of the knowledge that comes to me. I will do my best to live within the ethics of witchcraft, harming none and valuing myself and others. The Goddess is me and I am hers, body, mind, and spirit. So mote it be.

✳ Dip a small piece of the bread in the wine or juice, and eat it to seal your vows.

earning about the principles of magic, methods for raising energy, and discovering where magic comes from may seem daunting at first. Some books on magic assume a certain level of knowledge, or provide lengthy and sometimes confusing theories about how magic works. This chapter, however, makes it easier for you to grasp the concept of the magical web, existing within and around us, and enables you to become attuned to magic using some simple exercises.

Getting used to working with magic takes time, patience, and energy. The following suggestions for activities and exercises will allow you to experience what magic is and where it comes from. The activities are designed to extend your magical knowledge and help you to identify your place in the magical web. You will see in a new light, events, symbols, and images that you encounter every day, and discover some new ones along the way. This type of knowledge and building of ability will make your experiences in magic and ritual all the more powerful when you are ready to progress to circle work.

Participating in the set visualizations will enable you to build your own maps and identify personal symbols and reference points as you progress toward raising energy for spells and rituals. Most important, finding your place in the great web is part of your spiritual development as a witch. Locating the source of magic within and around you, and drawing these strands together, will help you to become a weaver of magical patterns. Starting from within, these patterns move outward into the wider web, causing subtle but powerful changes. This transformation is usually initiated by spells or rituals that partly mark and partly create, change. One of the most important sites of these alterations is within the self. Those who initiate change are always changed by it.

becoming magic

People begin searching for magic for many reasons. For some, it is a natural progression from an interest in exploring their spirituality; others may have been interested in magic since childhood. For some, it is a realization that they have abilities which cannot be explained away by so-called logical explanations. You may become aware of a kind of sixth sense, often cast as intuition, which tells you when the phone is going to ring, when close friends are in trouble, or which lets you read what is happening in situations, beneath the obvious content.

Whatever has drawn you to search for magic, learning to trust your intuition is the key to finding it. This is not always straightforward, as we are taught from childhood not to base our decisions on feelings. However, emotions are where magic begins. As we learn more about what particular feelings mean, we can work with the energies within and around us to produce magical results. Our ancestors who lived more closely with the rhythms of sun, moon, and earth found the relationship between feeling and action a lot easier. Industrialization and the coming of the Age of Reason has almost severed our connection to these energies so important to magic. Yet it is unnecessary to abandon technology in order to join with the cycles of the seasons and our magical abilities. Balancing both can be achieved with practice.

the magic of the moon

We can learn to connect with energies around us by using the changing phases of the moon. Begin by learning more about the moon, its effect on the tides and on the growth of crops. In the northern hemisphere, the moon waxes when it produces a sliver of light to the right-hand side, grows to full before waning away to a sliver on the left-hand side, and disappears at new moon. The effects that the moon has on the earth's vegetation and animals is well documented, but it also has more magical effects. Get in touch with your intuition and the rhythms of the moon by gauging its phases over a month. Keep a dream diary, noting vivid dreams and recurring symbols, either during dreams or waking hours. This way you can begin to connect with your inner abilities and natural energies.

linking with the earth

✴ Find a spot, outdoors or inside, where you will be safe and undisturbed for a while. Sit on the ground or floor in a comfortable position and close your eyes.

✴ Taking your time, concentrate on your breathing until you feel very still and very calm. Listen to your heartbeat and become aware of its pulse all over your body. Feel the pulse in your temples, throat, wrists, palms, knees, and ankles. Imagine another pulse, deep and slow, throbbing miles below you at the center of the earth. Feel yourself sinking through the ground or floor, drawn towards the deep heartbeat of the planet. Sink lower and lower until your heartbeat slows in time with the pulse of the earth. When you reach the center of the earth, your pulse becomes one with that of the planet. Stay for a while.

✴ When you are ready, slowly return to the room or place in which you are sitting. Stretch out and touch the things around you: grass or carpet, tree or chair. Eat and drink something to ground yourself after your journey.

✴ Practice this exercise often; you will gain confidence and it will flow more easily each time. Somewhere inside you, a little piece of magic is being enlivened, and that spark will set off the development of your magical consciousness, slowly but surely. Very soon, you will be ready to cast spells and perform rituals to do magic.

Developing your magical self is a gradual process, but it can be strengthened considerably by frequent meditation, visualizations, and exercises. These will stimulate your intuitive powers, and help you to identify what triggers such powers and how to put them into action. These exercises require a little patience and self-discipline but they really do work. They aid your concentration and breathing, and assist in building your ability to raise and direct energy. They are also good stress busters.

magical symbols

A way of enhancing your intuitive abilities is to learn about magical symbols and discover what meanings they hold for you. Some magical symbols are already quite well known. Many of us know which astrological star sign (sun sign), we were born under. All these signs have mythological figures and symbolic images attached to them, many of which were known and used by the ancients. Some of them were used by medieval alchemists who pursued the ultimate truth of the universe through working with metals and chemicals, all of which also had magical properties. Other symbols are found in the tarot, an old system of divination through numbers and archetypal symbols. Many of the archetypes found in tarot decks are recognized to have deep psychological and magical meanings.

Consider your birth sign and the symbol of that sign. If you are a Scorpio, you are represented by a scorpion, if Libra, a set of scales. What does the symbol of your sign represent about your own personality? For example, Saggitarians are represented by a centaur, half man or woman and half horse, who is also an archer. This can imply a jointly human and animal nature, one that always aims high and seeks enlightenment but is also earthed and grounded. Find out about the different stories associated with the symbols that depict your star sign. In which way do the stories and myths relate to you, your personality type, and your world view?

tarot

Try to get access to an illustrated tarot deck and study the major arcana, or the first twenty-two cards of the set. Before you find out their meaning, pick out the figure you are most drawn towards. Find out what your chosen card represents and meditate on its meanings. Consider why you were attracted to that card, and what it means to you now that you understand what it represents. When you have completed this exercise, look at all twenty-two cards together, and see if you can construct a story around the characters depicted there. The more familiar you become with standard magical symbols, the easier it will be to identify and understand signs in dreams and everyday contexts. This will increase your magical knowledge and boost your intuitive and magical abilities.

finding your magical symbol

✴ Lie down on your bed, and close your eyes. Relax, breathe deeply, and, when you are
ready, take one deep, lung-filling breath and release it slowly. Now you are ready to
begin an inner journey.

✴ Picture yourself walking through an open field in high summer with a gentle breeze
on your back and the warm sun on your face. As you walk forward, the season
changes around you and you notice the trees turning golden, then brown. Soon, the
wind becomes colder, the trees are bare, and snow begins to fall. Continue walking
forward across the snow. The changing seasons continue and there is a sudden
thaw. Before you reach the edge of the field and enter the woods to your left,
snowflakes and crocuses are already appearing. When you enter the woods, it is
springtime and bluebells carpet the ground. Walk through the woods into a circular
clearing. This is the space between the worlds, a place beyond places, in a time that
is not a time. Pick up a large stick from the ground and hit the nearest tree trunk
hard three times. This is to summon your symbol.

✴ Whatever comes into the clearing, stand still and accept it as your magical symbol.
Stay with it a while. When you are ready, return to your bedroom, and relax.

✴ Your symbol may be animal, vegetable, or mineral. Whether it is a fox, an oak tree, or
a hammer, it holds a clue to the nature of your magical abilities, which will be
revealed in good time. Find out more about your symbol. Look it up in world
mythologies, dream dictionaries, or even fairy stories. What is this
animal/plant/stone famous for? Find or make a representation of your symbol and
keep it close by. Look out for your symbol over the next month, in dreams, or in
everyday life. Meditate upon your new power symbol frequently; it will offer guidance
in building your magical skills.

magic within

The capacity for doing magic lies within us, and acting upon this knowledge involves becoming magic ourselves. Enhancing our abilities requires being conscious of the links between our inner and outer realities, as magic takes place on both planes. Part of a witch's work is to ensure the balance and matching up of these realities. This entails developing a clear awareness of what is going on in the world, on a local, global, and universal level. Discovering the magic located within requires a certain amount of practice before you are able to unlock your inner abilities.

It has often been remarked upon that many Western magical revivals borrow from Eastern religions. It is equally true to say that wisdom travels across cultures, and that on our spiritual journey we are rediscovering what people further along the path have already found all over the world. Witches in the West have always been aware of the advantages of meditation, even though this took the form of spinning, milking, digging, or fire gazing. We may not have spoken of "day dreaming" as a specifically magical or spiritual practice, but its value has long been recognized. Similarly, witches have been aware of their ability

witches in the west have always been aware of the advantages of meditation, even though this took the form of spinning, milking, digging, or fire gazing

to call up energy, even if we haven't had names for the energy points that become active in the making of magic.

One of the ways that we can call up the magic within us is to consciously energize these points. The following exercise will help you to become aware of and use these energy points more effectively in magic and ritual. In the East, these are known as "chakras," and each has a different name. You need only recognize them as inner locations that can be awakened to receive and raise energy. You will need to know how to wake your inner senses whenever you are involved in circle work. This will help you to get the best from the magic that you weave and the experiences you have within the circle.

Lighting candles and incense prior to carrying out this exercise will help create a calm and supportive atmosphere.

awakening your inner energies

✵ Sit on the floor in an upright position. Close your eyes and focus on breathing slowly and evenly for a space of fifty heartbeats.

✵ Picture your spine as a transparent tube, with openings at its base and the crown of your head. As you breathe in, visualize the column lighting up from the base to the crown, and as you breathe out, fading from crown to base again. Practice this a few times until it happens automatically.

✵ When you are ready, on the next breath in, picture a ball of red light brightening up inside your body at the level of the base of your spine. On your outbreath, the red ball should stay lit.

✵ Next, breathe in and visualize a ball of orange light inside your body at belly button level. Again, and with each subsequent energy point, this ball of light will stay lit on the outbreath.

✵ On the next breath, picture a ball of yellow light at solar plexus level. Proceeding upward, on the next breath, visualize a ball of green light at heart level. Take another breath, this time visualizing a blue ball of light at throat level. Next, visualize a ball of purple or violet light in the center of your forehead.

✵ Finally, picture a cascade of irridescent white light coming from the crown of your head and showering your whole body. Visualize this energy, for that is what it is, falling around you and then being drawn in again by the opening located at the base of your spinal "tube."

✵ Continuing this visualization, be careful to note how the different energy points feel during the exercise. When you are ready, visualize the procedure in reverse, turning off the lights beginning at the crown and ending at the base of the spine.

✵ It is important to eat and drink something when you finish this exercise, as this helps you "close down" again. If you don't, you risk leaving yourself too open and sensitive to emotions and energies around you. This can lead to emotional exhaustion and imbalance, and is to be avoided.

✵ Owing to the physical and powerful energies awakened during this exercise, you may find yourself feeling sexier than usual—this is quite normal.

Repeat this exercise as often as you can, until you raise energy without having to stop and think about it.

Now that you have begun to locate, identify, and awaken the magic within you, it is time to find the magic in the outside world, and to link these together. Magic is everywhere in the world, even in our towns and cities, the workplace, and the home. However, it is often easier to begin "tuning in" to outer energies somewhere green and pleasant.

Find a natural place where you can spend some time sitting and tuning your senses to the life around you. Listen to the birds calling to each other and watch them treehopping. Carefully observe the insects, earthworms, and spiders, and think about the different life forms that inhabit this place. Rest with your back to a tree, and imagine its sap rising, and its roots tapping into the deep earth to draw moisture and nourishment. Within this setting, there is a deeper pulse, a spirit of place that draws energy from all that lives there. This includes you, as you are now part of it. Mentally invite the spirit of the place to come to you. It is a different type of consciousness so it will not speak to you in words. Be prepared to pick up on emotions and feelings, and try to open all your senses in order to perceive its presence. If you are lucky enough to be contacted by the spirit of a place in this way, reciprocate with a mental "thank you."

You may wish to continue your relationship with your chosen place. You can do this in a number of rewarding ways. You might want to nurture the relationship by visiting it,

now that you have begun to locate, identify, and awaken the magic within you, it is time to find the magic in the outside world, and to link these together. Magic is everywhere in the world, even in our towns and cities, the workplace, and the home

taking care of it, clearing litter, and encouraging other, like-minded people to go there with you. If you have children, or younger sisters and brothers, you can take them on picnics there, play games there, or arrange outdoor activities that help them to learn about nature. It may be possible to do open-air rituals there at festivals and magical points of the year. Beltane, the time of green fertility, is an ideal time to stay out in the woods until dawn. It is also a good time to decorate your special place by "tree dressing" or making sculptures from natural materials.

The next step in finding and connecting with all the magic around you is to locate it in your everyday surroundings. Magic resides within the spaces between concrete and yards, street lights and front doors. You simply have to be ready and willing to find it. The following exercise will help you to make contact with magic, and, in turn, to find the sources of magic all around us.

discovering the magic around you

✹ Ensuring that you have complete privacy, locate a place in your home that is either physically central or that you sense is the "heart" of the house. Sit down on the floor at that spot, close your eyes, and relax. Slow your breathing.

✹ When you are ready, picture in your mind's eye the room in which you are sitting. Imagine that you are moving from room to room, picturing the details of the spaces you are moving through.

✹ When you have visited all the places in the house, return to the spot in which you are physically sitting. Picture yourself slowly shrinking until you are so tiny that fibers in the floor coverings tower high above you like trees. Picture yourself rising above the floor, and flying around the room you are in. You can see dust motes floating through the air, spider webs, and patches of dust in corners that look as big as islands. Spend a while seeing your surroundings from the perspective of someone only a hundredth of an inch high.

✹ Resume your position and go out into the street. Picture yourself growing until you tower above the highest buildings around you. Your neighborhood looks like a model village, the houses so tiny you could hold them between your fingers and thumbs. Spend a little while looking around at the streets, trees, and houses. Begin to rise high above the landscape, so that your town looks like a map. Spend time observing patterns and shapes in the land spread out below you, along with its hills, mountains, lakes, and rivers.

✹ Shrink down to normal size and return again to your house. Now mentally invite the spirit of your home and neighborhood to communicate with you.

✹ Consolidate this exercise by spending time making sacred spaces in and around your home to honor its *genius loci* or spirit of place. You can decorate different spots with plants, stones, or candles, or recycle everyday disposable things to create something beautiful. Place decorations at a spot that you wish to make special.

visualizing the web

Webs, mazes, labyrinths, and wheels are all ancient and potent magical and spiritual symbols. They depict the mysteries of life, death, and regeneration. Mazes, for example, provide passageways to and from a center, just as a cobweb is a spiral based on spokes, which can be traced inward and outward again. Circular symbols such as wheels, spirals, and labyrinth shapes were all representations of cyclical existence long before humans discovered that these echoed the shape of galaxies and DNA strands. The ancients intuitively drew upon these shapes to express their sense of time and place. Just as the greenery of the earth was constantly dying and renewing itself, so humans and animals also died, to be replaced by their descendants. The cycles of death and rebirth were constantly reasserting themselves, and people who had a closer relationship to the earth recognized this as a never-ending process. The symbols that best recorded that process were circles, spirals, and mazes, and sometimes snakes that swallowed their own tails.

witches include in their personal web all our relations, which means all things that have spirit. For us this includes trees, rocks, rivers

Witches use the great web of existence to explain our sense of all things being joined together. It gives us a strong sense of continuity and change, and helps us to understand our own place in this process. The web links the personal with the political, events with change, and all of us to each other.

Those who have tried to construct a family tree will understand just how effective the web is as a symbol of our place in the world. Even tracing your origins back two generations produces a huge web of blood ties. If you add to this friends, acquaintances, neighbors, and work colleagues, this web of personal connection spreads out enormously.

Witches include in their personal web all our relations, which means all things that have spirit. For us this includes trees, rocks, rivers, and different locales that have a spirit of place. Our web is the web of the home, the neighborhood, the land and everything in it, the sun, moon, stars, and the wider universe.

You can begin to find your place and sense of the web by casting your imagination inward and outward. The following exercise will help you catch at the threads of the great web, and expand your consciousness of your own spirituality.

meeting the spinner

- ✴ Find a place in your home where you will be undisturbed, and sit on the floor in the center of the room. Close your eyes and slow your breathing. Relax completely.

- ✴ Visualize a tiny silver spider on the ceiling above your head. Picture her spinning and weaving a gigantic silver web, with spokes spanning outwards to cover the whole room. She spirals swiftly around the room, spinning threads and linking them with the spokes, moving faster and faster until she is a blur and the room is covered with the web. She does this in each room in your home.

- ✴ She then moves to the front door, which opens. Follow her outside. In the sky is a gigantic web, stretching from heaven to earth. The spider joins your house web to the much larger web.

- ✴ Catch onto one of the threads linking the earth to the sky, and allow it to pull you upward, toward the moon. When you get closer to the moon, you will notice that it is really a huge spinning wheel, operated by a beautiful woman, dressed in black. She turns her face toward you, and you notice that her eyes are completely silver and her face expressionless. This is Arhianrod of the Wheel, the spinning goddess. She points outward into space.

- ✴ Beyond her, you see a gigantic maze with millions of people moving through it, traveling toward the center and outward again in constant flow. As you watch, the maze changes and turns to a gigantic web. The spokes of the web fade, leaving the spiral that joins them together. This spiral is made up of people, rocks, trees, rivers, streams, stars, planets, black holes, and empty spaces. It spins and grows smaller. When it grows infinitesimally tiny, it explodes. The matter it produces moves successively outward and spins back into a spiral shape.

- ✴ Turn back to Arhianrod, who offers you another length of silver thread. You take it and gently return to the room in which you are sitting.

- ✴ When you are ready, open your eyes.

- ✴ The thread presented to you by Arhianrod is curled up somewhere inside you, waiting for you to draw upon it when you need to remind yourself that you are connected to the great web of all life.

inner maps

Many people notice that in dreams we often return again and again to particular places. These can be either amalgamations of places we have actually been to, or places that we do not recognize outside dreams at all. These are part of an inner landscape, which is a wonderful world where cryptic messages concerning our innermost desires are sent for our conscious selves to unravel. It is also the place where our dealings with the everyday world are translated into symbols and stories to be sifted through in dreamtime. Our inner landscape is a place where magic can take root, and in which our magical and spiritual selves can come out to play.

imagination

The inner landscape is the place of the imagination. Imagining something is often taken to mean that what you saw or heard was not true. However, the word "imagine" has a far more important meaning than this. To "imagine" means to actively "image" pictures and symbols in your mind's eye that better encapsulate an object or concept you are trying to better represent or understand. An example of how an active imagination can

it is probably true to say that no two people's inner landscapes are the same. Just as people's appearance, personality, and experiences differ, so too, do our inner worlds

aid problem solving is a complex situation in the workplace "imagined" in a visualization as a series of knots in a piece of string. These knots are identified and untied one by one. This allows the person in the midst of a complicated situation to simplify it and identify resolutions. Active imagination can also be therapeutic: hypnotherapists often use it to reduce stress by talking clients through visualizations that encourage them to imagine the stress as a kite tied onto a bridge and then left behind them or a brick dropped into a river. Imagination (or "image-ination") therefore plays an active part in designing and exploring our inner landscape.

maps and systems of the inner self

The ancients actually tried to produce maps of inner landscapes. The very old Hebrew system of the Cabala, in which divinity is divided into ten spheres, provides a map of paths between them, which many witches interpret as a map of our inner divine selves.

Although this system can be considered to be universally applicable, it does not suit everyone. Other systems also provide guidance on inner worlds. Craft traditions that honor the Celtic tree alphabet, known as BethLuisNion, use this as guidance to our inner landscapes. Similarly, systems of symbols, including the runes of Nordic traditions, are used for guided visualization and meditation.

It is probably true to say that no two people's inner landscapes are the same. Just as people's appearance, personality, and experiences differ, so, too, do our inner worlds. The advantages of using magical systems are that they help us to access the different places inside our heads. They can sometimes be inspiring and help us to discover new spaces, ideas, and abilities. Alternatively, we can choose to rely upon our own intuition and begin to think our own way around the inside of our heads, guided by our dreams and our feelings.

myths and fairy tales

Fairy tales and myths are good ways of unlocking the power of our imagination. If we people our inner worlds with figures from these stories that seem appropriate to us, we have easier ways of encountering different parts of ourselves, and then linking these with our spiritual and magical experiences. Sometimes following old myths can produce some uncanny results. I once found a detailed description of a place that I thought I had invented in my own head, in a reproduction of a medieval manuscript I had never seen before. Significantly for me, being a witch and a pagan, it was a description of a location described by villagers as the abode of a nature spirit, said to rule over the beasts and trees.

dreams

Over the course of a month, try to record the places you frequent in dreams. Take note of common features appearing—houses are sometimes highly symbolic of the condition of your life or health at the time of the dream in question. Different rooms in a house can indicate different aspects of your life, and the state of the house is often a sign of the way things are going, and how you are coping emotionally with life. The sea is the archetypal symbol of the emotions, and paths can be indicative of directions you are taking. Try to link their occurrence with what is going on in your life, and start to explore your inner landscape in more active ways, for example, through visualization and meditation.

finding a patron deity

Having a goddess as a patron has advantages in terms of your spiritual and magical development. You may see it as energy, symbol, metaphor, an ancient entity, or simply a part of yourself. It is important that you draw upon the right goddess for this time in your life. Luckily, it is hard to do otherwise, unless you are feeling particularly willful.

There is a tradition in the Craft that holds that you get what you need, rather than what you are expecting, when it comes to gods and goddesses. If you are a spirited and independent personality expecting a patron goddess like Artemis, a powerful "maiden" deity, this may not be what you get. Your patron may well be Isis, the Mother of All, or Kuan Yin, goddess of compassion. Sometimes fiery souls are more in need of calm logic to check their sometimes irrational behavior rather than a fire deity to stoke up their already flaming personality. However, just because you are a quiet, gentle sort of personality, this does not necessarily mean that you "need" stoking up with an energetic fire deity. You may find a new manifestation or meaning to gentleness in Hecate, the wise.

The following exercise will help you to discover your patron deity. You may choose to do some research on different goddesses prior to this exercise but experience shows that it makes little difference to the outcome. What you may need to do is to study stories,

cherish this relationship; its effects will be felt for years after you step upon the path of magic and witchcraft

myths, and depictions of goddesses afterwards. Most people ask how they are going to know which goddess comes to them if they have little knowledge of gods and goddesses. The goddess in question will give you clues as to her identity; if she doesn't actually give you her name—it is always worth asking. It is up to you to investigate these clues afterwards, and find out more about her. Commune with her often in the circle or in visualization, in order to find out more about her and yourself.

After this first meeting, you will find your goddess in the everyday world, in symbols, events, your senses, and sometimes even in the landscape around you. Some people find it comforting or empowering to attain or make an image of their patron deity. They may use it as something to represent her in their home, or as a pendant to wear around their necks. This will help you forge a relationship that connects and balances your inner and outer landscapes. Cherish this relationship; its effects will be felt for years after you step upon the path of magic and witchcraft.

meeting your goddess

✳ Find a spot, outdoors or indoors, where you will be undisturbed for a while. Make yourself comfortable, slow your breathing, and close your eyes.

✳ Imagine yourself sinking deep below the bed or floor where you are lying or sitting. Picture yourself traveling through the layers of flooring, the foundations of the house, the cold earth, and the water beneath us.

✳ Sink further toward the earth's center, where it is warm and everything is lit with a red glow. Go deeper still and sink into the warmth of the earth.

✳ Imagine opening your eyes in a dark cavern, with tree roots for rafters above you; the hollow in the earth around you is lit with a warm glow. The roots you see are the roots of Yggdrasil, the world tree. Its roots go deep into the earth.

✳ Before you stands a table, upon which is set a blank piece of paper, an inkpot, and a quill. Walk over to the table and sign your name on the blank paper. When you have done this, knock three times on the table and mentally invite your patron goddess to appear to you.

✳ Sit on the floor of the cavern and watch as the table, pen, ink, and paper fade and disappear. To your left is a doorway, covered by a deep blue veil. Your patron deity will enter through this doorway.

✳ When it comes into the room, take careful note of its appearance, including anything it may be carrying or wearing.

✳ If your patron does not offer its name at first, you may ask it. Take note of any clues that it offers to its identity.

✳ When this stage of the exchange is over, you may then ask a question. Once you have received your reply, thank your god/dess and return to the place in which you are meditating.

The next step after becoming magic is to do magic. This chapter sets out the basis for casting spells and working ritual by introducing you to the traditional systems on which spellwork is based. It will also guide you through the principles of magic, traditional tools, ingredients, and practices.

Just as computers need instructions written in a particular language in order to respond correctly, the magical web needs its instructions in language it can understand. Witches have to communicate effectively in this language in order to do spellwork, and we do this by using a "code" that enables us to tap into the appropriate resources from within and around us. The "code" is actually very simple. It helps us to condense our wishes into symbols that we can use in spells. Consequently, casting a spell means sending out our intentions in concentrated form; a spell is really a sort of pattern guide for magic to work with.

The place for casting spells and working rituals is within a magical circle. The "circle" is a marker of the sacred space in which we do magic.

In addition to this framework of symbols, there are two complementary systems that govern timing. The first is based on the cycle of the moon. The second is a system associating the days of the week with certain planetary influences. Like the elements, the planets preside over aspects of existence, such as communication, love, and health. In witchcraft, timing particular spells to coincide with the most fortuitous day and moon phase is considered crucial to effective spellwork.

Casting spells is the activity most commonly associated with modern witchcraft and attracts the most curiosity and sometimes fear from the public. This is because of common misunderstandings about the nature of magic and the ways in which spells work.

Magic is something that is constantly within and around us. Witches come to accept it as part of everyday life, and of nature. When we cast spells, we are weaving these energies into a new pattern. This is part of the witches' craft. Weaving with nature means you cannot go against nature and although magic can achieve some wonderful things, it cannot create miracles. Witches do not have power over life and death.

the five elements

The main basis for spell casting and ritual in modern witchcraft is the system of the five elements: air, fire, water, earth, and spirit. This has ancient origins, and has been used in the past to help doctors understand human physiology and philosophers understand the basis of existence. In witchcraft it is used in meditation, spiritual attunement, and magic. It provides us with correspondences—symbols associated with and representative of the five elements of life. These are used in spellwork to represent our intentions toward the person or event that the spell is focused on. Using this system helps us translate those intentions into the appropriate magical "code."

Over the next few pages, you will be guided through visualizations in which you will meet the five elements. These are exercises that can be repeated often, and expanded upon as your experience takes you further along your magical path. These need to be treated as essential rather than optional parts of your path into witchcraft; by experiencing the elements for yourself, you will be able to fully appreciate their significance in witchcraft.

The five elements of magic are: air, fire, water, earth, and spirit. These are also the elements that make up all life. In magic, the elements rule over different aspects of our lives, and provide symbols that help us to key into them.

air

The magical meanings attached to the five elements are closely related to their functions in the physical world. Air, for example, is the first element we encounter as we draw breath for the first time at birth. The physical properties of air mean that we send our speech out into the world on an outgoing breath, and it is vibrations in the air that create sound. Not surprisingly, air has come to be the magical element associated with communication. This has been extended to embrace all forms of communication, whether spoken, signaled, written, or electronic. Since we package a great deal of our ideas and thinking into speech or writing, air is also seen as the element of thought, ideas, and learning. Other forms of communication are also represented by air: travel, commerce, examinations, legal litigation, and publishing.

fire

Fire is represented by the power of the sun, from which we draw warmth, light, and energy. It is experienced within our own bodies as the electricity that sparks our cells into life. In other contexts, fire is experienced as the different forms of energy that power technology. It is also used to sterilize or purify. In magic, fire is the element that rules over different types of energy, both physical and metaphysical. In the circle, fire represents courage and willpower, loyalty and faith, as well as physical energy. Fire presides over matters of success, well-being, creativity, energy, confidence, inspiration, and action.

water

Water is present in our bodies as tears, milk, and blood, and in the wider world as the deep oceans. Our bodies produce tears when we are happy or sad, milk to feed our children, and blood when we are injured or menstruating. In magic, water represents the emotions, nurture, healing, love, and fertility. The tides of the sea are caused by the moon's gravitational pull, and so water is closely associated with the lunar cycle. Water as a magical and physical element is tremendously important to all life on this planet.

earth

Earth is present all around us in the form of the physical planet, soil, seabeds, mountains, and plant life. Within our bodies, it is present in the form of our bones and teeth and the minerals that keep us healthy. In magic, earth represents the material world, health, wealth, and all forms of physical manifestation. In the circle, it is associated with material needs such as shelter and food, and presides over property, protection, stability, and growth. Earth spells are for prosperity and other material means of support.

spirit

Spirit, which is not present physically in a single identifiable sense, is what unites the other elements together to give them shape and being, and so represents transformation. In magic, the element of spirit is often envisaged as a web, with its many spirals and connections representing the strange cycles and coincidences that shape our lives. Spells invoking the element of spirit are usually for spiritual growth and transformation, and are cast by those seeking to learn more about magic through personal experience.

enhancing your magical abilities

The five elements system is easy to work with once you are familiar with it. The following exercises initiate a closer connection to the elements. After each exercise, you will be more aware of the nature of the respective element in the everyday world, and of its meaning in magic. This promotes a much closer working relationship with the elements, and helps to enhance your magical abilities. These exercises will help you build on your present abilities and prepare you for the adventures in magic awaiting you further along your path.

air

Air is traditionally the first element to be honored in a magical circle. It is positioned in the east, the place of the sunrise, and is linked to beginnings of all kinds. As we know, air is associated in magic with communication. It is also associated with movement and travel, probably because it is the natural element of birds.

Not many of us consider the importance of air to our everyday existence and we usually draw breath without thinking. Yet the oxygen in the air we breathe is the fuel that feeds all the cells in our bodies.

experiencing air

When you are out and about, notice the effects the wind has on trees, on water, and on buildings. If you have good hearing, try changing the tone and volume on your radio or stereo and become aware of the wide variety of sounds that can be produced. You can experience the vibrations that produce sound by striking objects and touching them, or placing your body next to large stereo system speakers carrying a loud bass beat. Try speaking or reciting in front of a lit candle, and watch the flame flicker at different rates as your tone and volume vary. Make or buy some wind chimes and hang them in your garden or porch—listen to the wind as it moves through the chimes. Find new and exciting ways of experiencing that other gift of air: scent. Bring scented plants and flowers into your home or try burning incense or essential oils when meditating—cone, stick, or loose incense is widely available in today's "specialty stores." Watch birds in flight and observe their patterns as they fly in formation, and the way they use the air currents and therms to gain height, hover, or land.

breathing

Try spending five minutes being conscious of drawing breath deep into your lungs and expelling it. Imagine the air coming into your lungs and inflating them, and your lungs deflating as they expel it again. Try taking a deep breath in through your nose, imagining it is the first breath you have ever taken. When you breathe out through your mouth, imagine that it is the last time you will do so. Spend a little time thinking about how this feels to you, and what air means to us as humans.

In preparation for the following visualization, spend time becoming aware of your breathing in the way described above. See if you can gather some of the symbols for air: a wand, a feather, images of birds (particularly owls), the planet Mercury, Hermes, messenger of the gods, the color yellow, sunrise, springtime, Athena the goddess of learning, incense, citrine crystals, or pine trees.

meeting the element of air

✷ Find a space where you will be undisturbed for at least 30 minutes. Sit or lie in a comfortable position and close your eyes. Spend time slowing your breathing until you are completely relaxed and ready to begin your inner journey.

✷ Imagine that you are standing in a field at the top of some cliffs. It is sunrise, and you can hear the sound of seagulls and the waves crashing against the beach far below. In the field there are four tall stone gateways each facing north, east, south, and west. Walk toward the eastern gate (nearest the sunrise), and pass through it. As you do, you feel a peculiar sensation beginning at your shoulders and running down your arms. When you look at them, you notice little stubs, rapidly growing into feathers. You watch delightedly as your arms turn into swan's wings with feathers of all colors. When the transformation is complete, you beat your wings and leave the ground. You quickly find that you can fly even higher. Explore the air, rising as high as you dare, swooping above the field, over the clifftops, and above the sea.

✷ After a while, you notice that the wind is growing stronger. Fly into it and allow it to carry you away. The wind carries you into a whirlwind, that blows away your feathers and lifts you higher. It whips at your hair and makes you feel fresh and alert. Problems and troubles fall away and everything seems clear. The wind drops, and you float gently down into the field. One of the birds feeding in the field has a message for you attached to its foot. This message consists of one word and only you will understand its significance.

✷ Lie down in the field and close your eyes. When you are ready, return to the room or spot in which you are meditating, and open your eyes.

✷ If the message you receive is not immediately meaningful, you will come to understand it within a moon of carrying out this exercise.

fire

The second element to be greeted in the circle is fire. It is positioned in the south, the position of the sun at noon when it is at the height of its powers. Fire is associated in magic with energy because it is seen in the solar energy that brings life to the planet. It is also experienced in the energy that fuels technology and the many electrical charges that energize cells in our bodies.

The sun, the ultimate manifestation of fire, is something we are frequently aware of. If the day is dull, we complain about the lack of sun and notice that the people around us tend to be more miserable than usual. We often use the sun to symbolize happiness in songs, poems, and everyday language. Someone has a "sunny" nature, or when bad luck strikes, we reassure them that "every cloud has a silver lining." It is likely, then, that you are already aware of the importance of the sun as something that affects our psychological state. Certain people in the northern hemisphere even suffer from Seasonally Affective Disorder, or "winter blues," a form of depression linked to a lack of sunlight in winter.

experiencing fire

Try to notice the different senses in which fire is important to us. One gift of fire is light: turn off all electric lighting, unplug the TV, and sit in candlelight for one evening. How does this affect your evening's activities? Another gift of fire is heat; go camping and leave the stove behind. You will probably find that a real fire becomes a focal point for cooking, warmth, and company in the evening. Consider how important fire was to our ancestors, who relied upon this form of energy. Practice building and maintaining a bonfire in the open air: working with fire and keeping it "fed" is a good way of getting to know fire in its most primitive form.

warmth

On a sunny day, spend a few minutes sitting in the sun. Become conscious of its warmth on your skin, and visualize the sunlight being absorbed through your skin, tissues, muscles, and bones. Think about what the sun means to life on our planet and to humans in particular. Consider the ways in which fire is important to all life, and the many ways in which the energy of fire is used.

Use all of these activities as preparation for the following visualization. Meditate on the magical symbols for fire and try to collect together one or two prior to the exercise: images of flames, a dagger, lanterns or lamps, the color red, Brigid the goddess of Fire and inspiration, yellow dandelions, candles, the planet Mars, horseshoes, the noonday sun, summer, or oak trees.

meeting the element of fire

✴ Find a space where you will be undisturbed for at least 30 minutes. Sit or lie in a comfortable position and close your eyes. Concentrate on the warmth of your body, and allow yourself to relax.

✴ Imagine that you are standing in complete darkness. A tiny dot of light in the distance begins to grow and you realize that something is rushing toward you. The object is a large flame, and when it approaches, you experience a brilliant light and a rushing heat. The flame passes through you, leaving you feeling energized and warm. Gradually, it grows lighter and you find yourself on the hot sands of a tropical beach. The sun is high in the sky, and in the jungle you can hear birds and creatures calling through the undergrowth. In the near distance is a smoking volcano, which occasionally rumbles and shakes the ground. Stay a while in the heat of the sun.

✴ After some time, you notice that further down the beach there is a long black and red oblong shape in the sand, and that the air above it shimmers with heat. You walk toward it, and find that it is a pit of glowing coals. The sand that you have already walked upon is very hot, but this pit is glowing red. Breathing in deeply, drawing in strength from the sun through your solar plexus, gather your confidence and step onto the hot coals. Feel the fear build and fall away as you walk the length of the hot coal pit. You do not burn, but gather in energy as you walk on the glowing embers.

✴ Spend some time walking through fire and enjoy the feeling of power and strength that comes from it. When you have finished, step onto the sand and sit down, facing the volcano. Close your eyes and relax. When you are ready, return to the room or spot in which you are meditating, and open your eyes.

✴ Hopefully, you will have brought some of the energy drawn from the element of fire back with you. Repeat this exercise whenever you need confidence or strength, or feel lacking in energy.

water

The third element to be welcomed into a traditional circle is that of water. It is positioned in the west, the place of the sunset. In magical terms, water represents love, healing, and balance. Its association with emotional matters comes originally from ancient Greek wisdom which held that water was the one of four humors present in humans that held the key to balance. The physical properties of water, which always finds its own balance, tend to support this link.

Two fifths of our planet's surface is covered in water and most scientists agree that all life on earth began there. As individuals, we float in water in the womb for nine months, growing and evolving in preparation for life after birth. It is not surprising, therefore, that water also represents change.

experiencing water

If you can, spend a day by the sea, watching the waves and the changes of the tide throughout the day. Find some large, dry pebbles or stones and pour water over them. Notice how the water changes their appearance and brings out hidden depths of colour and textures. Go for walks in the rain, or run a shower just for the sensation of water pouring over you. Visualize all the problems of the day being washed away by the water. Meditate and relax in a candlelit bath, with rose-petals floating on its surface. Make a water feature in your home; this can be as simple as a glass bowl of water with floating candles, or a more sophisticated indoor water fountain. Try to visit the local swimming pool or beach more often, and get used to submerging yourself in water.

water for life

Taking time out to meditate, close your eyes and become conscious of the blood coursing around your body. Imagine your pores pumping out sweat and your mouth becoming dry. After five minutes, open your eyes and fetch a glass of water. Sipping slowly, imagine your body rehydrating, the water entering and balancing your system. When you have finished, imagine that your body is the earth, and your veins are the rivers that feed the soil and flow to the sea. Think about the many ways in which our existence is owed to water, and what happens when there is no balance, when there is drought or flood.

Use these activities as preparation for your guided journey to meet the element of water. Before embarking on the following exercise, consider some of the symbols of water and try to gather together one or two: a goblet or cauldron, shells, glass pebbles, a mirror, images of the sea, fish, the planets Venus or Neptune, Aphrodite the goddess of love, the color blue, sunset, the moon, stars, fall, apples, blue stones, or willow trees.

meeting the element of water

✳ This exercise is best carried out lying down on a bed. When you are in a comfortable position and completely relaxed, close your eyes.

✳ You are lying on your back, eyes closed, on a sandy beach. It is late afternoon, and the air around you gradually grows cooler. You listen to the waves lapping at the shore and the distant sound of birds. When you open your eyes, the first stars are beginning to appear in the sky, and the moon has already risen. As you sit up, the sun begins to dip below the horizon. When it has completely set, you watch the vast expanse of water before you. As it gets darker, you notice an object floating toward you from a great distance. You see that it is a small wooden boat, with a dragon's head carved in the prow. You wade out to meet it, noticing how cool the water is around you, and climb in. The boat turns and carries you out toward the horizon. Dusk is setting in but the moon is bright enough to pick out schools of fish and the occasional flash of fin above the water's surface. The boat speeds on until you lose sight of land, then slows down until it is still, moved only by the ripple of the breeze on the sea. You dive into the sea and swim down until you reach the seabed.

✳ At the seabed, you find that breathing holds no problems for you, that your eyes adjust to the darkness, and your body does not bob back up to the surface. Walk on the seabed and meet the dolphins, rays, tiny darting fish and colorful squid that swim by. After a while, you come to a large gray limestone rock. The buoyancy of the water enables you to pick it up easily. Something is embedded in the rock. Move closer and examine it more carefully. This "something" is a gift for you. Make sure you note it in your journal.

✳ When you are ready, return to your bedroom and open your eyes.

✳ The meaning of the object embedded in the rock is for you to decipher; it will help you to understand the significance of water.

earth

The element of earth is the fourth to be welcomed in magical circles. It is placed in the north, the position of the sun at nighttime. Earth represents material things such as solidity, physicality, and manifestation. It is the element in which plants and crops are able to grow, and it has come to represent the fertile land, with its positive associations of physical provision, wealth, and property.

Many of us are conscious of earth in the form of our planet because of the threats posed by pollution. A distorted perception of "wealth" as private or corporate capital gain has resulted in climate change and rising sea levels, which threaten both land and people. The Old Norse people referred to the riches of the earth as "wealth and weal." This was a much healthier perception of both "earth" and "wealth" as it referred to need, sufficiency, and anything extra as a blessing from the earth. In magic, earth offers us stability, plans coming to fruition, and physical well-being.

experiencing earth

Try getting outdoors more often and spend time in green spaces such as parks, gardens, or even the countryside. The presence of trees and greenery has a calming effect and can be spiritually uplifting, but have you thought about the wider function of the planet's trees and greenery? Trees are the lungs of our planet: they absorb carbon dioxide and produce the oxygen so important to our survival. They provide homes and food for much of our wildlife, and their growth records geophysical events that have taken place in the planet's history. Their roots can help prevent subsidence in areas susceptible to mudslides. Planted closely together, trees also provide shelter from the wind for tender crops.

nourishment

If you do not already have any, bring some plants into your home and "green" your living space by sharing it with growing things. Make a meal entirely from root vegetables, grown in organic soil. Become more aware of your body, what it needs for fuel, how often it needs rest. Take care of your physical self. Stretch, exercise, and massage your skin with nourishing creams or oils. Consider the physical makeup of your body—the minerals it needs in order to function and where these might be obtained.

All of these activities will prepare you for the visualization that follows. Think about some of the symbols for earth and see if you can gather some prior to the visualization: a stone or wooden pentagram, crystals or rocks, images of mountains or planet earth, Demeter, goddess of the harvest, ears of wheat, mosses, the color green, midnight, winter, bread, salt, or oak trees.

meeting the element of earth

✴ Find a spot where you will be undisturbed for at least thirty minutes. Sit in direct contact with the floor or ground, close your eyes and relax.

✴ You are sitting in a forest clearing at night. It is lit only by the stars and you can just see the outline of the trees against the sky. Unseen animals move through the branches and in the undergrowth. As your eyes become accustomed to the darkness, you stand up and make your way to an opening to your right. It is a pathway, and as you make your way along it, you notice the baked-dry mud beneath your bare feet. You become aware that you are approaching a rockface. The path stops, and it appears to be a dead end. As you move closer, however, there is an entrance to the rock, a low tunnel set close to the ground.

✴ You kneel down and crawl into the darkness. After crawling for a little while, the tunnel opens up to allow you to stand. Soon, the tunnel begins to twist and turn, and take you downward. As you continue to descend, you notice a faint green glow coming from the walls. Occasionally you catch a glance of phosphorous mosses, and as you move forward, it begins to grow lighter. The tunnel leads to an enormous cave deep below the earth's surface. It is hot, and the cave is filled with terracotta oil lamps. In the center of the cavern is a bubbling pool of mud, oil, and steam. The ceiling is vaulted with the vast roots of an ash tree. This is the World Tree. Sitting between some of the larger roots, at one end of the cavern, are three old women. They are veiled in black. One spins threads, one weaves, and the other cuts.

✴ One of them will stop and speak with you. You can ask her one question about the element of earth. The answer is for you alone. When she has finished speaking, thank her, and let the vision fade.

✴ When you are ready, return to the room or spot in which you are meditating, and open your eyes.

✴ Take note of which of the women spoke, as this has will come to have some magical significance to your path in the craft.

spirit

The fifth element is spirit, and it is traditionally the last to be greeted in a magical circle. It is positioned in the center, and is considered to be present everywhere. Spirit is the great alchemist of existence; as the element that unites all others, it has the power to shape the very nature of all things.

The usual sense of the word "spirit" in everyday life is that which is apart from the material world. In reality, transformation and interconnection, which are aspects of spirit, are part of everyday life. Sometimes we experience the spirit as the "chemistry" that makes a party successful, or the particular combinations that bring people together. However, "connection" should never be mistaken for "fate." Believing in "fate" makes people passive and superstitious; witchcraft is active and responsible.

experiencing spirit

Take a fresh look at how human life fits around our planet's arrangements in the solar system. Out of town, the moon and stars provide light at night, and the sun by day. We have water, out of which we came and without which we cannot grow or sustain life; fire in the shape of the sun and other energy; the air that we breathe; and the earth from which we are made and in which we grow food.

Observe the way that people behave towards each other, sometimes helping strangers, sometimes being unkind when it would have been reasonable to be helpful. We all have a relationship to each other, which may be good or bad. Think about your position in all of this: "spirit-uality" means discovering your connections with all others, and your place and purpose in the universe.

relationships

When you have five minutes, sit and meditate, think about the connections that have brought you to study witchcraft. What are your life choices right now and where might they take you? Study the night sky and learn about our own solar system, beginning with our planet, moving out to its relationship with the moon and the sun, and then the other planets. Spread your net wider to incorporate your relationship to all those you come into contact with on a day-to-day basis. Learn more about where our planet is in relation to the rest of the known universe.

These activities will prepare you to meet the element of spirit. Spend time thinking about the symbols of spirit and try to assemble one or two prior to the exercise: spiders, webs, Hecate goddess of witches, crossroads, the moon, spinning wheels, spirals, corn dolls, weaving, the color purple, cords, clear quartz crystal points, or cypress trees.

meeting the element of spirit

✴ Find a space where you will be undisturbed for at least thirty minutes. Sit or lie in a comfortable position and close your eyes and relax.

✴ You find yourself sitting on a hillside beneath a night sky. Lying with your back to the earth, you see the constellations of Orion, with the three stars of his belt, and the Pleiades, or "seven sisters" like a brooch to the west. Venus shines close to the moon, whose disk is totally eclipsed by the shadow of the earth. The sky is unusually clear and to the east, there are meteorite showers. Slowly, you begin to rise above the earth, high above the hillside. Below you, towns' lights glitter and diminish. You continue rising, until you see the seas and oceans. Soon, you are floating high above the earth, outside its atmosphere, and see it as a huge sphere in space. You begin moving quickly outward, past the moon, past Mars and the outer planets. When you are outside of our solar system, you slow down and float in the depths of space.

✴ After a while, you notice a bright flare in the darkness. This is a new galaxy being born. Watch as it explodes and spirals outward, flinging debris from its center. Some of the larger rocks it throws out eventually stop moving outward, as they are caught in the gravitational pull of a bright star, around which they begin to orbit. As they revolve around it, they begin to rotate. Some of them have satellites or moons. One, the third rock from the bright star, changes from red to blue. It has a large single satellite that revolves around it, reflecting the light of the star onto the planet. You begin to float toward this planet and, as you descend, recognize it as home. You float slowly back down to your hillside, to watch the night sky lighten as the moon sets and the sun comes up.

✴ When you are ready, return to the space in which you have been meditating. Your journey through space and time will become meaningful as you progress on your magical path.

casting a circle

In witchcraft, spells, rituals, and celebrations are carried out within a magical circle. This circle marks the boundaries of the space set aside for these purposes. The shape of the circle symbolizes the cycles of life and death experienced, eventually, by all things in existence. It therefore has a spiritual as well as a magical significance to witches.

The most common questions asked about the circle concern its boundaries, its construction, and the etiquette for moving about in it. The answers to these questions are obvious once you experience circle work for yourself, but there are some initial pointers. Once you grow accustomed to casting and working in a circle, you can afford to be more experimental. In the meantime, work with this basic system until you are confident enough to try something new.

The circle is not physically drawn on the floor but is formed instead by the energy raised and directed through the person that casts it. This energy is sent out through our bodies, directed through an athame (witches' knife) or index finger, to "draw" or "describe" a circle in the air around the room. Often this is envisaged as a line of white or pale blue light and is cast "deosil" or "sunwise" (clockwise). The circle, once cast, is envisaged as rotating around both vertical and horizontal axis in order to form a sphere; this is still referred to as "the circle."

Circles are cast deosil and when raising power, it is customary to move around in the circle in that direction. This applies when you are getting ready to raise power in ritual or in spellwork and means that you should avoid getting up and walking around it "widdershins" (or counterclockwise) at the wrong time.

The following exercise shows you how to cast a circle. Drawing energy in order to create a circle isn't difficult, but you will need practice in becoming aware of the energy points in your body. You will also need the experience of the circle to learn about different energy levels; this takes time and practical application is the only way to achieve it.

preparing your space

✴ The best time for casting a circle is after sunset. Find somewhere you can work undisturbed for an hour. Identify the four points of the compass by orienting yourself around the places of sunrise (east) and sunset (west). With the sunrise to your right and sunset to your left, you are facing northward, and south is behind you.

✳ Place a candle for each of the elements in secure holders at the appropriate points: yellow for air in the east; red for fire in the south; blue for water in the west; green for earth in the north; and purple for spirit in the center. Have ready a wine glass of water, and a pinch of salt in an eggcup.

"cleansing" the space

Saltwater is a traditional purifier, and is used to psychically cleanse a space prior to the casting of a circle. Here, the water is "neutralized" so it can carry the magical properties of salt.

✳ Directing all your concentration through your hands, lift the wine glass in both hands, and visualize the water being emptied of energy. At the same time, say: I empty you and prepare you to receive the purification of salt, that you may aid me in my work.

✳ Take the salt and bless it saying: I bless you in your task of purification. May you cast out all that is unneeded so that good may enter in. Pour the salt into the water, and sprinkle this around the room.

casting the circle

✳ Stand in the center of the compass points, and energize your energy points as indicated in the exercises in the previous chapter. Direct energy through your solar plexus, down your writing arm, and through your index finger. Send out the energy, visualized as a bright light, through your finger and visualize drawing a circle in the air large enough to encompass the space that you are in. Visualize the circle rotating and forming a sphere with yourself the center.

✳ Light the element candles, beginning with air, moving deosil through fire, water, earth, and spirit at the center. Spend time sitting in the circle, experiencing the stillness and the shifts in energy.

✳ When you are ready to close the circle, visualize it fading away. Blow out the candles in reverse order beginning with spirit. Stamp your feet on the ground several times in order to "ground" yourself. Concentrate on closing down your energy points a little, and take something to eat and drink, as this will help the process.

self-blessing ritual

You are now ready to start working ritual and magic. The following ritual is a self-blessing and a declaration that you are ready to take your first steps on the path of witchcraft. The different features of the ritual are explained to help you plan your own rituals in the future.

rites of passage

Most newcomers are puzzled by the terms "ritual" and "spell" and wonder if they are just different terms for the same thing. Strictly speaking, they are not. If we define "ritual" as meaning a series of actions that are symbolic and embody certain intentions, we can see that this does describe spellwork to an extent. However, rituals, unlike spells, are symbolic enactments for celebrating, marking, or putting into effect, all sorts of life changes. This may include rites of passage such as birth, death, menopause, old age, or spiritual transformation, and so, although spells are rituals of a kind, rituals are not necessarily spells.

creating a ritual

Creating a ritual begins with the setting up and marking out of sacred space, that is, casting a circle. What happens next depends on how simple, or complex, you wish to be.

It is customary to welcome the elements with a few words before lighting the appropriate candle, after the circle is cast. You can say something simple like: I welcome the element of air; you are honored in this circle. Alternatively, you may wish to customize your welcome for a particular occasion by mentioning something of the quality you wish each element to bring to the ritual. In a ritual for spiritual and magical growth, for example, you may wish air to bring the gift of "clarity" and so on.

Once the elements are honored, it is usual to state the purpose of the ritual. This is a powerful signal to the magical web that something is about to happen.

symbolization and planning

All ritual is real life, or real intentions, dressed in symbolism. One of the most important things you have to establish is how you are going to represent these. Symbolizing objects and articulating events is easier if you consider how they are represented within the system of elemental correspondences, and the systems for timing used in witchcraft.

First, you should consider timing. Guidance on working with the ebb and flow of magical tides along with the days of the week and their correspondences is given further on in this book. This will enable you to identify the best time for your ritual.

Second, consider the element. If you have started working with the elements, you should already be expanding upon further correspondences as appropriate to each.

Third, you should identify ways of symbolizing the people, objects, and events to be represented in the course of the ritual. For this, you will need to consult elemental correspondences and use a little imagination. Ingredients for rituals and spells need not be expensive or rare; stir your creative spirit and see if you can find ingredients in the kitchen cupboard, the sewing box, or the garden shed.

self-blessing ritual

preparation

✳ This ritual is best carried out on a dark (new) moon as this is the most auspicious time for entering a new magical phase. The element for transformation is spirit, so the ritual is carried out before the purple spirit candle in the center of the circle.

ingredients

✳ Conduct this ritual naked. You will need a teaspoon of salt and a teaspoon of carrier oil (almond or grapeseed) containing approximately two drops of cinnamon oil and one of benzoin, both oils symbolizing fire (initiation) and the sun (success).

the ritual

✳ Cast a circle in the usual way. When the spirit candle is lit, sprinkle the salt on the ground in front of it and step onto it. Say aloud:

> I choose this path of my own free will, I am willing to learn, I am willing to grow, I ask the blessing of the goddess of the witches, by all her names, known and unknown.

✳ Dip the fingers of your writing hand in the oil, and anoint your body at your feet, your womb/lower abdomen, heart, lips, and third eye, saying each time:

> "Blessed Be."

Sit and meditate in the candlelight, then close in the usual way.

enchantment

"Enchanting" involves chanting or singing as a way of energizing a charm or spell. To "en-chant" means to chant your intent into something, and is an important method of power raising used in witchcraft. To enchant an object is to charge it magically with power raised through the rhythmic repetition of a simple phrase in speech or music. Chanting is often used in witches' circles as a way of raising energy. The act of chanting keeps the rational, controlling part of our brain busy, leaving the part, we believe, that governs intuition and psychic power free to do its work. At the same time, the rhythm of chant lulls the rational side into letting go.

uses of enchantment

How enchantment is used in witchcraft varies from place to place and group to group, and it can be adapted to fit different purposes. If a spell is being cast by a coven, the group may choose to chant together and pass around a particular object to direct the power they raise to the end they wish. Sometimes chanting is used in conjunction with dancing, or moving together deosil around a circle. The power of sound is often used in the act of healing, and chanting is a highly potent force used in this type of magical work.

Another use of enchantment is to prepare an object to be used in spellwork or circle work by magically energizing it. In the case of candles, this can be done for a number of purposes. Candles can be prepared either for general use in lighting a circle, for element candles, or in candles to be used for spells.

making magical candles

Candles enchanted for general circle use add a special dimension to a circle. If you have made them yourself, it adds a personal touch, and enhances the atmosphere at rituals. Element candles can be enchanted with the energy specific to the element in question. For a yellow air candle, for example, you should use a chant associated with air, and visualize the magical properties of air as you charge it with that power. An ideal chant would be: "Wearing my long tail feathers as I fly, (Repeat) I circle around, circle around the boundaries of the earth." You can, of course, choose to make your own chants. Candles to be used in spells can also be enchanted with the potential to receive wishes and then release them when lit.

How, then, does one enchant a candle? The answer is very simple. One quick and very easy method is to hold a candle in both hands and chant at it, willing the energy raised from the chant to move into the candle itself. Another, more powerful way is to enchant the candle as you are dipping it.

dipping candles

To enchant the candles as you make them, chant as you dip. This way, the candles are empowered layer by layer.

ingredients

✳ A tall jug, cold water, old newspapers to cover the work surface, a tall glass jar, several packs of natural beeswax candles, a large saucepan, a stove, candle dye (available from most hobby stores), essential oil (optional), long-handled fork, and sheets of clean white paper (one for each candle).

method

✳ Place the jug, filled with cold water, on newspapers to the side of the stove.   Place the jar, filled with household candles, in the saucepan. Fill the saucepan with hot (but not boiling) water as high as possible without the jar becoming unstable or floating.   Place the saucepan on a lit stove, and bring the water to boiling point. Allow to simmer.

✳ As the candles in the jar melt down, add more candles until the jar is filled almost to the top with molten wax.   Add candle dye if you are making candles of a specific color.   Add an appropriate essential oil if you wish them to be scented.

✳ Using a long-handled fork, remove all the wicks from the molten wax and place them in the jug of cold water.   Place the wicks to one side for future use. Take one wick and dip it in the molten wax, then in the cold water in the jug.   On lifting it out of the water, you will see that the wick now has a layer of wax.   Shake off the water and put it back in the wax, and then in the water.   Repeat these actions, keeping as much water off the growing wax candle as possible when it is removed from the water.

✳ When the candle is large enough to sit comfortably in a candle holder, roll it on clean paper to smooth the surface of the wax.   Leave to harden.

timing

The timing of spells, rituals, and other celebrations is considered with great care in witchcraft. We use timing correspondences as part of sympathetic magic, and the criteria we use for pinpointing the appropriate times complements the framework provided by the five elements system.

concept of time

When considering time, we have to acknowledge that the human concept of time is socially constructed. Our calendars have changed at various junctures in history, and they differ the world over. It is also thought that our sense of time has shifted over thousands of years from cyclical—associated with the cycles of the sun, the moon, and in the agricultural era, crops—to linear—time ordered into sequential stages in history. The limitations and definitions we place on time are symbolic rather than natural. Although we may be accustomed to twelve months lasting thirty or thirty-one days, the moon tends not to respond to a calendar we have divided up for our own convenience.

A witch's concept of time is slightly different from the conventions with which she is generally surrounded. As people who consciously strive to reconnect with nature and the cycles of change, we divide the solar year into more organic markers with our eight festivals. Similarly, we draw upon our spirituality and pagan customs in linking days to planets. The most important cycle we work with in magic is that of the moon, our nearest celestial neighbor.

the moon and spellwork

One lunar cycle, the time it takes for the moon to revolve around the earth, is 27.32 days. During that time, although the moon keeps the same face turned toward us, it goes through different "phases." These phases are the apparent changes of the shape of the moon from dark (new) to full and back again to dark. The moon does not actually change shape; it is the way that the light of the sun is reflected by it according to its position in relation to the sun and the earth. The lunar cycle affects sea and ocean tides on earth, which are mainly due to the gravitational pull of the moon. They are also related to a lesser extent to the sun. At certain times, when the pull of sun and moon are combined, they lead to stronger tides, for example, in the spring.

In magical terms, we recognize the coincidence between physical and psychic phases and tides. The lunar phases are used in magic for different purposes. The dark moon is used for matters of protection, banishing, diminishing, and restrictions. It is seen as a "time out of time," which is particularly potent. The waxing crescent, through to half, gibbous, and then full, is used for growth, attraction, and drawing things toward you. The full moon is sometimes considered a quieter time magically than most people imagine, as some magicians consider the moon to have been "completed," literally fulfilled and at a standstill. This does not mean that nothing goes on at full moons; these are used for the Esbat, or monthly gathering of circles and covens. If you work alone, you may wish to use the full moon to celebrate your spirituality, commune with your gods and/or goddesses, seek guidance from the tarot or runes in the circle.

The waning moon, from the day after full, through gibbous, half, and back to the final crescent, is used for banishing, exorcising, diminishing, or repelling. These phases of the moon in the northern hemisphere are seen in the sky as waxing from right to left until full, then shrinking until the last crescent is seen on the left hand side of the moon's disk. A waxing half-moon is lit on the right hand side, and a waning half-moon on the left.

The principle of moon magic is very simple. Cast spells for increase and attraction when the moon is growing, those for decrease or banishing when it is shrinking.

energies

It is important to remember that there is a finely tuned relationship between the symbolism of certain timing, and the actual energy changes that occur at particular times. Whereas the system used for the days of the week functions more as a symbolic framework that has changed over time, the phases of the sun, moon, and seasons carry particular energies with them. Witchcraft attunes with these energies in an intuitive sense.

astrology

The nuances of certain cycles are expressed particularly well in the realm of astrology. Our sun-sign is said to be the aspect of our natal chart that most influences our true personality, whilst our moon-sign represents our emotional side. In magic, the moon cycles are especially important as they relate to emotions and intuition, both of which are natural components of our magical selves.

days of the week

Different traditions of magic stipulate different times for certain spells. Some types of highly ceremonial magic, for example, divide the hours of the night into planetary correspondences, and specify that the climax of a spell coincides with this hour. The system used here is based on the days of the week, and their correspondences. These are based on ancient pagan lore and provide a simple system that complements the five elements.

personalities

All of the days of the week have "characters," as though they were personalities rather than markers of time. These are useful as a guideline to what sort of spell you might cast on a particular day. Just as the elements have a color scheme, the days of the week also have associated colors. Each day has a ruling planet and a corresponding metal. There are traditional planetary symbols associated with the days. Nontraditional symbols are drawn from witchcraft associations and astrological traditions.

sunday for success

Sunday is named, naturally, after the sun. Its character is bright, happy, healthy, and fortunate. The type of spell you might cast on this day would be spells for success, contentment, happiness, good health, and fortune. The planetary symbol for the sun is a circle with a dot in the center—this also functions as a symbol for Sunday; the "sun's day." The metal and color associated with the sun and with the day itself is gold, the symbol of spiritual fulfillment in alchemy. Another symbol of Sunday is a sunburst.

monday for money

Monday is named for the moon. Its character is psychic, mysterious, alternative, and emotional. The types of spells you would cast on Monday would be those related to psychic ability, emotional issues, balance, and mental stability, and, according to tradition, money in the form of cash. The planetary symbol of the moon is a disk showing the moon in any phase, usually crescent. Both the metal and color for Monday is silver. The image of the moon in its late crescent phase is another symbol of the moon and Monday.

tuesday for protection

Tuesday, named after Tiew, Celtic goddess of Ploughs and reputed mother of Lugh, a solar deity, is characterized as fierce, assertive, impulsive, and inspiring. Ruled by the planet Mars, Tuesday is the day for spells for protection, assertiveness, confronting bullies, and seeking energy. Its associated metal is iron and its color is red. Its traditional symbol is that of Mars, and is used to denote maleness—a circle with an upward-pointing arrow. Another symbol for Tuesday is an upward-pointing dagger, sword, or spear.

wednesday for communication

Wednesday is named for Woden, chief god of the Saxons. Wednesday is characterized as being quick, communicative, intelligent, and knowledgeable. This day is ideal for spells to do with communication, vehicles and travel matters, legal issues, house sales, examinations, and memory. Its ruling planet is Mercury, and this is also the name of the metal associated with it, sometimes known as "quicksilver." Its traditional symbol is the astrological sign for Mercury, and it is symbolized by the color yellow. Another symbol for Wednesday is a wand, or caduceus (a wand encircled by two snakes).

thursday for justice

Thursday is named after Thor, the Norse god of thunder. Associated with the planet Jupiter, Thursday is characterized as generous, just, and friendly. Spells for good fortune, charities, justice, and property matters are best cast on this day. Its symbolic color is purple and its metal is tin. Thursday's symbol is the same as for that of its ruling planet, Jupiter, though a less well-known one is that of scales fronted by a hammer.

friday for love

Friday is named after the Norse goddess of love, Freya. This day is characterized as beautiful, affectionate, harmonious, and loving. Friday is ideal for spells concerned with love, friendship, beauty, self-image, and harmony. Its color is green, and its metal is copper. Friday is symbolized by the traditional astrological symbol for Venus, its ruling planet, also known as the symbol of femaleness—a circle with a cross beneath. A lesser-known symbol is a scallop shell.

saturday for banishing

Saturday is the day of Saturn, known as the planet of old age. It is characterized as slow, forbidding, silent, and effective, and it is the best day for spells of binding, banishing, and diminishing. It is associated with the color black, and the base metal, lead. Its traditional symbol is that of the planet Saturn, or sometimes a lantern, which in the tarot is generally carried by the Hermit.

Until you become familiar with these correspondences, it is useful to draw up a chart listing them, and put it somewhere you are likely to see it at odd moments so that you can begin to memorize it. Alternatively, you may wish to hang up a chart in the place where you are most likely to meditate or plan magical work.

magical tools

Regarding the requisite number and type of magical tools, witchcraft traditions tend to differ. Some stipulate numerous tools that accord with a complex system of usage, while others take a much simpler approach. For the purposes of this book, we will work with those tools most commonly recognized by witches the world over: the wand, athame, chalice, pentacle, and cords.

wand

The wand is the tool associated with the element of air. Wands are made from many types of natural materials, including crystal spars, but are generally carved from any wood of choice; traditionally hazel and willow. Wands range from about 7.1 inches (18cm) in length to solid 10 feet (3m) high staffs, according to personal choice. If used in circle work, they are used to direct energy. Some witches forego the use of a wand; while others keep it as a purely symbolic object rather than an active magical tool.

athame

The athame is the most common tool to be found in the witch's repertoire. It is a dagger or knife, usually black-handled, and it is used to direct energy, normally when casting a circle. Today, athames are available through mail order from pagan cutlers, either complete or self-assembly with blade, handle shaft, and separate pommel. The latter form of athame allows you to make your own handle from a substance of your choice and to empower the athame by putting all your personal energies into its making. Traditionally, the athame is taken outdoors, thrust into flame, dipped in water, and plunged through the air into the earth.

chalice

The chalice is used very often in magical circles, especially at Esbats and Sabbats. It represents the element of water, and is linked with other legendary vessels, such as the Arthurian Grail and the Cauldron of Ceridwen in Welsh mythology. It is a tool of healing and communion with others, and is used both in magical spells and in offering wine or juice among participants in group circles. Chalices are made from a variety of materials, including glass, clay, and silver. Traditionally, your chalice should be given to you as a gift. This tradition has been altered a little over time and it is now considered appropriate to buy your first chalice once someone else has presented you with a cup of any sort. If you wish to follow this convention, you may consider using a nice glass of some sort until the signal comes to choose your own special chalice.

pentacle

The pentacle is a powerful symbol in witchcraft, the five points of the star representing the five elements. When this pentagram is encircled, the sign represents earth. The pentacle is usually a disk inscribed with or marked by a five-pointed star (sometimes encircled). It is placed in the earth quarter or, more usually, on the altar. It is used to bear the bread or cake shared at the end of rituals. The pentagram or "platter" can be made from any natural material, but it is usually made from wood or clay.

cords

Cords, representative of spirit, are generally placed on the altar. These are the initiation cords of a witch, symbolically representative of her life as a witch. Placing them in the circle commemorates the promises she has made to herself and to her sisters and brothers in the craft. These are never used in magical spells and are never unfastened or damaged. Other types of cords may be used in spells for witches' ladders or bindings.

obtaining your magic tools

Ideally, we could all carve our own wands, make our own athames, cast or glaze our own chalices, fire or cut our own pentagrams, and weave our own cords. This is not always possible, and it is perfectly acceptable to purchase them. By tradition, however, one should never bargain for or haggle over tools bought for magical purposes. This is the price we pay for relying on the talents of others to supply our magical tools.

alternative tools

A magical tool can be defined as something you use in order to work magic; this includes ingredients and implements used in casting spells. If you do not yet have an athame, you can use a kitchen knife, a nail, pin, or needlepoint to inscribe symbols in wax. Similarly, you can use a bread board or marble cheese platter in place of a pentagram, and so forth.

assembling the tools of magic

Ingredients for spells can be found in the sewing box, the kitchen , tool box, office, or specialty stores. Once you have begun working with the five element system, and have assimilated the significance of moon phases and days of the week, you should find it easy to assemble the tools of magic in a way that make sense in your life. There is no need to obtain your definitive five tools all in one go, or wait until you have them all before you begin magical work. Be prepared to work with makeshift tools until you find those you consider special enough to consecrate and keep aside for magical use only.

incenses and herbs

Herbs and incenses have been used in magic for thousands of years. Modern witches probably have much less herbal knowledge than our ancestors, who lived closer to the land. However, of the population in general, no one, apart perhaps from the odd herbalist, knows more about herbal folklore than witches.

The use of herbs, flowers, and incenses in magic are symbolic and energy raising. There are many good books on magical herbalism, from which you can learn a great deal about herbs, incenses, oils, and flowers. This section is a rough guide to their uses.

magical incense

Incense is used to bless and consecrate the circle and enhance the atmosphere to make it conducive to the purpose for which it has been cast. It is also used to purify or banish negative energies during exorcism, "cleansing," or consecrating magical tools. Like oil, it is used to invoke particular energies to aid in rituals and spells.

It is thought that the first incenses used were dried berries, herbs, scented wood, and tree gum. Juniper berries are still used in Purification Incense, as are many types of herb, such as lavender or rosemary. The basis of most magical incenses today is granular gums such as frankincense, myrrh, or copal. Combined with dried woodchips, for example, red cedar or sandalwood, dried herbs such as sage, and flowers such as geranium or rose, and mixed with a few drops of an essential oil such as patchouli, these gums make excellent bases for protection, healing, love, or prosperity incenses.

burning incense

There are a variety of forms in which you can purchase incense. The most powerful and useful in magic, however, is loose incense, preferably mixed by yourself in preparation for particular spells and rituals. Loose incense is stored in jars and scattered onto a burning charcoal disk. These disks are inexpensive and available from many "New Age" outlets or through mail order. They are approximately 1 inch (2½cm) in diameter, convex on one side, concave on the other. When properly lit, they spark up and grow glowing hot. When the disk is red hot, the loose incense is scattered into the concave side of the disk, which should be facing upward, and scented smoke is emitted. As the lit disks grow hot, it is necessary to place them in a fireproof pot, such as a brass censer, and place them on a heat-proof base to protect the surface on which you place it. A safe, makeshift censer can be made from a terracotta plant pot, placed on a coaster, filled with earth and topped with some gravel kitty litter. There are also good censers available on the market.

herbs and flowers in magic

Herbs and flowers are significant ingredients in magic. They are used to make amulets or talismans to attract or ward off, respectively, certain energies. Rings of dried juniper berries sewn onto black thread, or bunches of rosemary can be hung over the front or back doors of a property for protection against burglary, for instance. Alternatively, you can scatter rose petals in a bath prior to a ritual for a love spell, or tie nasturtiums into a piece of muslin to be worn around your neck to guard against spiteful tongues or gossip.

essential oils

Oils are powerful in raising energy and are used in circle work in the same way as incense, that is, warmed on a burner. They can also be used to anoint the body or worn as a scent. Essential oils are easily available from specialty stores, and you can make your own blends in carrier oil, if it is to be used on the skin.

protection incense

Mix three parts frankincense with one part juniper berries (whole) and one part dried fennel or rosemary. Add three drops of rue or rosemary oil, mix thoroughly and place in a jar or plastic bag to blend for 24 hours. Burn on a charcoal disk.

passionate love oil

To be worn by those who wish love to come to them. Use 10 drops of carrier oil to each drop of essential oil. Mix three drops of geranium with three drops of vanilla and two of clove oil. Leave the oil to steep for seven days before use.

prosperity amulet

Make a small wreath (approximately 2 inches [6cm] in diameter) by carefully threading mint and basil leaves together and onto florist wire. Gather together some cinnamon sticks and drill a hole in them using a sharp needle or craft drill. Thread pieces of cinnamon on at regular intervals around your wreath. Hang on your front door to attract prosperity.

broomstick and cauldron

Two of the most compelling items in the iconography of witchcraft are the broomstick and the cauldron. They owe their origins to the fantasies of witchcraft accusations during the persecutions in Europe and have remained potent symbols of the witch's craft.

witches' transport

The broomstick, which along with the pointy hat and bubbling cauldron still form part of the archetypal image of witchcraft, does not appear in witchcraft iconography before the 15th century. Broomsticks, along with other long-stalked plants, were alleged to have transported witches through the air in order to attend upon the Devil at Sabbats.

thresholds

Broomsticks actually occupy a very different space in folklore. Generally placed over a front door or next to a hearth, they are seen in several ways to signify "thresholds" or places of transition. The expression "living over the brush" is still applied in parts of England and Scotland to couples living together without having married. This expression comes from the tradition of couples declaring their partnership before the community by jumping or stepping over a broomstick.

household use

It is likely that the broomstick gained its "threshold" reputation to a certain extent from common household usage, when it was positioned in key places around the home. However, the broomstick has, throughout its history, attracted a number of sexual connotations that give us a clue to its continuing use in contemporary witchcraft.

sexual metaphor

The conjunction of the yonic brush and the phallic broom handle are perhaps the basis of some of the other customs associated with it. Ancient Welsh legend tells us that Arhianrod, a goddess of renown, was challenged to step over a magical staff (rather like the handle of a broomstick), in order to prove her virginity. As she stepped over, she was shamed by suddenly giving birth to twin boys. One custom has it that virgins should not step over a broomstick handle, or they will be similarly shamed. In this tradition, the broomstick handle acts as the threshold between the truth and falsehood, maidenhood and motherhood, but also as a judge of sexual experience, past or future.

Contemporary witchcraft is quite fond of sexual metaphors and embraces the symbolism of the broomstick as a positive. It functions as a symbol of fertility and conjunction, thresholds and transitions. As a tool, it is used sometimes to prepare ritual space, by sweeping out negative vibrations or energies.

depraved brewery

Cauldrons are found in 16th-century woodcuts of witches' Sabbats, as part of the apparatus of the feasting and spellcasting that, it was alleged took place there. Some depictions show babies being cast into the pot, or ointments of foul ingredients being brewed. In fact, a cauldron was an important piece of kitchen equipment to have in medieval and early modern Europe. Since cooking often consisted of a variety of foods thrown into one pot on the fire, a sturdy cauldron was essential. In spite of the cauldron's reputation as the utensil for brewing magical concoctions, smaller pots were probably more economical for cooking up medicinal poultices or herbal teas. Nevertheless, the cauldron has come to represent the vessel of depraved brewery in the annals of diabolical witchcraft.

regeneration

Magical cauldrons abound in myth and legend, and some pots discovered by archaeologists are thought to have had sacred significance in the prehistoric, ancient, and Dark Ages world. A magical cauldron appears in the Mabinogion, a book containing Welsh myths. It is depicted as an instrument of regeneration, where warriors slaughtered in battle, if placed in the cauldron, would rise up and fight again. Taliesin, a legendary Welsh bard, was said to have gained his wisdom from the cauldron of the goddess Ceridwen.

the modern cauldron

The Holy Grail of Arthurian legend, which was said to have contained the blood of Christ, is considered by witches to be a later, Christianized version of the magical cauldron of the earth-goddess. The chalice sought by the Knights of King Arthur was attributed with the power to heal the land, and it could be attained only by one who was "pure of heart." This legend echoes the custom of Celtic tribes who symbolically wed their male chieftains to the goddess of the land. The ceremony would then marked by a great feast, in which a communal cauldron was used.

The cauldron, in solid cast-iron form, is still used in witchcraft today. Usually, it is used to burn incense or contain fire in that to burn objects which need to be destroyed. Equal parts of Epsom salts and pure alcohol are used to set a fire in a cauldron, over which members of a coven may leap during festivals. The safety precautions here need hardly be emphasized. Many covens claim that the best use they put a cauldron to is for the meal served at the end of Esbats and Sabbats.

Rituals are symbolic enactments or representations of what is happening in your life, or what you wish to happen. Marking changes in your life in ritualized form, or making a ritual for life changes, sends out the message onto the magical web that you acknowledge what has happened, and are moving forward, or wish to.

Rituals can bring about a number of profound spiritual changes. As part of the web, you are always changed by acts of magic as much as the magical intent affects the outcome. In ritual, this is amplified, as you are making an acknowledgment in relation to where you are in your life, including your spiritual self.

Ritual has many functions in witchcraft and can be used for many different purposes. In your magical and spiritual development, there will be times when you wish to effect and mark change and transformation. These may include initiation into the craft, the taking or changing of a magical name, changes of direction on your magical or spiritual path, life events, and rites of passage.

The following sample rituals are concerned with aspects of your magical self, for consecrating and energizing tools, and celebrating and marking important moments in your life cycle. In addition, you will be offered guidance in constructing your own rituals. You will also be introduced to the ways in which rituals in witchcraft can offer alternative and more meaningful celebrations to the recognized markers of marriage, naming of newborns, birthdays, anniversaries, funerals, and memorials. You will also learn how rituals can add meaning to processes and life changes not generally acknowledged or celebrated in wider society, such as ending relationships, recovery from dependency or illness, menstruation, parenthood, grandparenthood, and retirement.

Rituals can be celebrated publicly or privately. The first two rituals are intended for celebration either alone or with others. Some occasions suit themselves to one rather than the other, while others are a matter of personal preference. Provided you do only what you are comfortable with and make balanced judgments about how others will react, rituals incorporated into a celebration party can a wonderful experience.

magical name

It is customary for witches to take a magical name at their initiation or you can take one when you are starting out in the craft. This name is part of your magical identity and it is important to choose the right one at the right time. You may wish to change this name at a future time to mark life changes.

There are various ways to find a name. One is to use a simple system of numerology, as in the table below. First add the numbers in your name to the year of your birth, until you arrive at a single number. Next, try to construct from the letters of the alphabet a name that has the same final number as your present name and year of birth.

1	2	3	4	5	6	7	8	9
A	B	C	D	E	F	G	H	I
J	K	L	M	N	O	P	Q	R
S	T	U	V	W	X	Y	Z	

$$A+N+N-M+A+R+I+E+G+A+L+L+A+G+H+E+R+1+9+5+7=$$
$$1+5+5+4+1+9+9+5+7+1+3+3+1+7+8+5+9+1+9+5+7= 107$$
$$1+0+7 = 8$$

As my number is eight, I can make up a name with letters that add up to eight:

$$K+E+Z+I+A+S = 8 \qquad C+E+R+I+D+W+E+D=8$$

Another method is to swing a pendulum over deity names. Your pendulum can be a terminated crystal threaded onto a chain or cotton, or a threaded needle. If your pendulum swings more over one or two names, test it over these until you can identify just one. This is your magical name.

ritual for taking a magical name

preparation
✴ This ritual should be carried out on a waxing moon.

ingredients
✴ A small slip of paper and a pen with purple ink. A sturdy incense burner, and two lit disks of charcoal, one on top of the other to maximize the heat produced. A teaspoon

of frankincense granules. Anointing oil, made from carnation petals steeped in carrier oil for seven days on a waxing moon, to which you should add one drop of honeysuckle essential oil to fifteen drops of steeped oil.

the ritual

✳ Cast a circle. Invoke the elements with the these words at the appropriate quarters:

> I call upon the element of air to bless my circle name.
> I call upon the element of fire to inspire me for as long as I go by this name.
> I call upon the element of water to consecrate my magical self.
> I call upon the element of earth to know my name as I walk upon the ground.
> I call upon the element of spirit to bless me in this task, and change me until I fit the name I have chosen.

✳ When the spirit candle is lit, pause for nine heartbeats, then go deosil around the circle, introducing yourself by your chosen name to the elements in turn, saying:

✳ My name is... ...know me by this name as I honor you in magical work, worship, and celebration.

✳ Stand before the spirit candle, facing north, and write your name on a small slip of paper in purple ink. Place this on the red hot charcoal disks to burn, then place frankincense granules to consecrate the name in the smoke. Anoint yourself with oil before the spirit candle, at your wrists, your heart, and third eye, saying:

> As the goddess blesses me by my new name, I use that name to bless myself, May I be known and blessed by that name as long as I carry it. So mote it be.

✳ Thank the elements and blow out their candles. The ritual is complete.

consecrating tools

A witch's tools need to be consecrated—made sacred for their sacred purpose. All tools, except the athame, should be blessed in the following ritual. Cords are only exempt if they have already been part of your initiation ceremony. You can do this ritual when you have assembled all of your tools, in which case you should not use any of them for magical purposes until this is done. Alternatively, you can consecrate them one at a time. A similar ritual can be used and adapted to bless any tools you wish to use for magic.

The athame is consecrated—purified and rendered sacred to its purpose—by being introduced to the elements during its making. If you wish to consecrate it again in the circle, you sprinkle it with salted water, anoint it with purification oil and pass it through incense smoke.

ritual to consecrate and bless magical tools

preparation
✳ This ritual should be carried out on or one day after, the dark moon. Prepare an altar and set out a censer, water, salt, and blessing oil around it. Light the charcoal disk.

ingredients
✳ A wine glass of spring water and two pinches of salt in a separate bowl. Loose incense made from white sage and juniper berries in equal parts, mixed with cypress essential oil to make it slightly tacky. Allow to steep for seven days prior to use. Blessing oil made from ten dried bay leaves steeped in five dessertspoons of carrier oil for seven days of a waning moon, with three drops of frankincense oil.

the ritual
✳ Cast the circle and welcome the elements, asking them to bring the following gifts:

Air: Bring to this circle the gift of knowledge, that the tools I bless may be instruments of learning.
Fire: Bring to this circle the gift of strength of will, that the tools I bless be instruments of my magical will.
Water: Bring to this circle the gift of compassion, that the

tools I bless bestow healing.
Earth: Bring to this circle the gift of manifestation, that the tools I bless bring wishes to fruition.
Spirit: Bring to this circle the magic of connection, that the tools I bless work patterns of transformation.

✳ Hold the wine glass of water in your left hand and, directing your energy through your right index finger, put the tip in the water and visualize all energies in the water departing, saying:

I exorcise this water, casting out and emptying it of all energies it has absorbed from this moment on.

✳ Take the salt and cover it with your right hand, saying:

I bless this pure salt that it may aid me in my work.

✳ Mix the salt with the water and bless it in the name of your patron deity. Take the tool you are blessing, and sprinkle it with the saltwater, saying:

I purify you with salt and water.

✳ Place the tool on the altar, and anoint it with the blessing oil saying:

As I bless you, you will bless all you touch.

✳ Sprinkle some incense on the charcoal disk and pass the tool through the smoke, saying:

Know all ye elements, this sacred
(wand/chalice/pentagram) as my instrument.

✳ Hold up the tool toward the five elements in and around the circle in turn. For an athame, pass the tool through the incense smoke saying:

Behold this sacred athame.

✳ Thank the elements for their blessings and close the circle.

life changes

Rituals for celebrating or marking life changes are an essential part of the spiritual path of witchcraft. Witches have become adept at creating alternative rituals for the more conventional rites of passage such as birth, marriage, and death. However, we also recognize a wider number of defining moments in human experience.

The life cycle and changes in it are made up from a number of different experiences, both social and biological. Marking these important times is a way of setting new values around them, as well as making them meaningful. Other, nonbiological events can be as equally life-changing. The end of a relationship, for instance, can be devastating. Putting our feelings into the framework of a positive ritual can help us to recognize and vindicate our grief, anger, or sadness on a number of levels.

Make a list of life changes or events that might be marked by a ritual. Choose one (but not the example given), plan a ritual around it, and then see how your ideas compare with the following ritual. This ritual is designed to sever all connection to a past relationship, and includes a role for friends to support the person performing the ritual.

ritual to mark the end of a relationship

preparation
✳ This ritual is carried out on a waning or dark moon, preferably on a Saturday after dark.

ingredients
✳ A black candle, a photograph of the ex-partner, two 9 inch (25cm) lengths of black cord, and a chalice filled with water.

the ritual
✳ Cast the circle. Light the black candle at the center of the circle, saying:

> Saturn, planet of restriction and banishment, I call upon you to witness how I (name) sever myself from (name of ex-partner).

> Hecate, goddess of crossroads, I call upon you to watch over me as I choose a new direction.

✳ Ask your friends in turn to confirm their willingness to help you in your task.

> ## (Friend's name): are you willing to help me break from the past and move onward?

When both have answered Yes, you answer:

> ## I appreciate and value your friendship.

✳ Hold up one of the black cords in front of the black candle and say:

> ## This is my link to (ex-partner's name).

✳ Tie a knot a third of the length from one end, and another knot a third of the length from the other, the first is for you and the other, for him/her. Hold the knot for your ex-, saying:

> ## This is (ex-partner's name); I free him/her and wish him all he/she deserves.

✳ Hold the knot that is you, and say:

> ## This is me; I free myself and wish myself all I deserve.

✳ Cut the cord in the center, holding your knot. Your friends now take the other length of cord and each tie a knot, close to the ends. You tie your knot onto the center of this piece, saying:

> ## Until I recover, I rest on the support of your friendship

✳ Hold up the photograph and the cord with his/her knot in front of the black candle, saying:

> ## (Ex-partner's name) I commit you to your future, and cast you from mine, I dissolve all commitment to your emotional welfare.

and burn them both in the candle flame. Place the ashes in the chalice to be poured onto soil away from your house after the ritual.

all occasions

For more conventional rites of passage, such as births, marriages, and deaths, the "big three" markers in our lives, there are a number of ritual outlines already in existence in covens, groups, or on the Internet. Their variety demonstrates the flexibility of ritual, once you have an established framework that sets a space and time, and provides appropriate symbolic representation, you can fit it to meet any requirements.

The following ritual celebrates a "handfasting," or a pagan "marriage." The framework offered here is endlessly adaptable, and is found in many different forms throughout the witchcraft world.

ritual for handfasting

preparation
✳ Place lit nightlights in jars around a circle approx 13 ft. (4m) in diameter. Use seasonal greenery to decorate. Tie the rings to a cushion and place on the altar. Light an appropriate incense. Place a broomstick near the entrance of the circle.

the ritual
✳ The couple enter the circle and join hands. The officer for air speaks and lights a candle:

> **These are the blessings of the element of air; may you always share ideas, tell each other your dreams, appreciate each other's intelligence. The gift of air is communication.**

✳ The officer for fire speaks and lights a candle:

> **These are the blessings of the element of fire; may you always find inspiration in each other, find the energy you need to support each other, and have faith in your relationship. The gift of fire is passion.**

✳ The officer for water speaks and lights a candle:

These are the blessings of the element of water: may you offer each other compassion, may you wash away hurts and share each other's joy. The gift of water is love.

✴ The officer for earth speaks and lights a candle:

These are the blessings of the element of earth: may you never want for food or shelter, may you thrive in health and enjoy the good things of the earth. The gift of earth is the material world.

✴ The couple light the spirit candle on the altar. Reader one reads a poem chosen by the couple. Musicians and singers play a song chosen by their friends. Reader two reads an extract on love chosen by the couple. The couple ask each other:

I am willing to declare my love for you and my commitment to our relationship. Are you willing to do the same?

✴ When each answers in the affirmative, they exchange rings saying:

I offer this ring, symbol of unity and eternity, as a token of the love I am declaring here today. I offer with this ring my own commitment to you, my loyalty and my love. I promise to be a good partner for as long as love lasts.

✴ The officer of water and the officer of earth toast them in turn, saying:

May you never thirst. May you never hunger.

✴ The couple step toward the broomstick at the front of the circle, holding hands, saying:

Let us be married, let us be wed, by crossing of broom and the joys of the bed.

✴ At this point, the couple jump over the broomstick.

The following spells come from a mixture of ancient and modern traditions of magic. You are advised to follow the instructions for timing very carefully. If you need to adjust some of the ingredients, consult the elemental and/or planetary correspondences.

There are some general guidelines to be observed when casting spells to ensure safety and effectiveness.

✴ Make sure that what you are doing is needed and is not a substitute for other types of actions and responsibilities.

✴ Ensure that you are undisturbed while you are in the circle as it is important to keep your concentration on the task at hand.

✴ The circle can be cast with an athame, a wand, or your index finger, provided that you direct and visualize the energy coming through either.

✴ At the end of a circle, remember the elements you have honored and blow out all the candles.

✴ When a spell is cast, you can choose to remain in the circle a while longer if you wish to meditate or commune with your deities. When you have finished, if the energies of the circle have not started to fade (practice will enable you to feel changes in energy levels), you should "ground" yourself by stamping on the ground, and visualize the circle as fading away before you leave it.

✴ Circles are cast all around the room in which you are working, so you should not leave the room for the duration of a circle.

✴ All element candles can be blown out at the end of spell-casting and reused for other spells and rituals. Although some guidelines advise against this, there is no real reason why you should not recycle in this way. Candles used as part of a spell are usually left to burn completely down in a place of safety, unless extinguishing it is part of the spell, in which case directions as to its safekeeping and disposal are stipulated and should be observed.

✴ Take safety precautions at all times, and have a fire extinguisher, or water bucket on hand in case of accidents with candles or incense burners. Ensure that candles are placed in secure holders and stand away from drafts or curtains and draperies.

earth magic

Earth is the element most associated with the material world, and its powers are suited to spells that are concerned with the "solid" issues such as food, shelter, and income. Earth is seen to rule matters related to our bodies and our continued physical prosperity. However, it also has another magical property: that of protection. Earth offers protection against anything that threatens the integrity of property, body, or physical well-being.

This spell for protection is based on an old tradition of sympathetic magic, which represents like with like. Just as a hedgehog or porcupine presents its quills to the outside world if under threat, this spell is based upon the principle of using sharp objects to represent the power we wish to wield if threatened by harmdoers. Spikes, needles, thorns, teeth, and metal nails were once used in charms to repel troublemakers. These were buried in jars as a protection against trespassers, burglars, unwanted callers, or unpleasant neighbors.

Some traditional spells tend to emphasize the weaponry aspect of this protection, and advocate the burial of iron bars or hammers in the garden. This version of the spell uses the traditional iron nails placed in a glass jar. Although this is predominantly a protection spell and not a curse, some of the words are adapted from an old Saxon curse that describes the conditions under which harmdoers are bound.

the "spiky jar" spell

preparation
* This spell should be cast on a waning or dark moon, after dark, on a Saturday, which is ruled by stern Saturn, planet of discipline and restriction. The green and black candles should be placed in the center of the circle or on the altar and the Protection Incense lit prior to the circle being cast.

ingredients
* A green candle, anointed with patchouli oil. A black candle, anointed with almond oil. If possible, a few cactus spines and thorns from hawthorn or rose trees. A screwtop jar, thoroughly washed and dried. A handful of iron nails, at least ¾ inch (2cm) each in length. Protection incense, made from one part sandalwood chippings, one part dried thistle head, two parts dried rosemary and two parts juniper or mistletoe

berries, with one drop of St. John's Wort (hypericum) oil per dessertspoon dried mixture.   A square of plain muslin, large enough to wrap around the jar. A 6 inch (15cm) length of household string.

the spell

✳ Cast a circle, welcoming the elements and lighting the element candles. Light the green candle, saying:

> I call upon the element of earth to watch over, bless and energize this spell of protection.

✳ Light the black candle, saying:

> Saturn, old one and wise, repel and banish harmdoers from my door and my hearth, send away unkind ones, those who wish to steal or damage and all who threaten me and mine.

✳ If you have managed to obtain cactus spines and thorns, put them carefully into the jar. Take the nails and hold them up in your right hand in front of the candles, face north, and say:

> By this good metal and with these points I forbid harm-doers to approach my door. May all that approach with evil in their hearts be bound from doing harm. May they be bound by a straight line and a crooked, on land and on water, living or dead. I return to them all their deeds, good and bad. So mote it be!

✳ Pass the nails over the incense smoke. Place the nails in the jar and seal it tightly. Cover the jar with muslin and tie this tightly above the lid, using the string. When the circle is closed, bury the jar as soon as you can in your front or back yard, or in a pot containing soil in your yard or apartment.

air magic

Spells carried out under the auspices of air are usually concerned with an aspect of communication. Air is also seen as swift, facilitating, and intelligent, and is the perfect patron for spells involving movement, for example, to a new home, country, or job.

There are many deities in pagan traditions associated with air. Its main archetype in alchemy is Hermes, messenger of the gods. This figure is associated with the planet Mercury, which travels around the sun in 88 days. The goddess most associated with air is Athena, goddess of wisdom and learning. Her totem is the owl, a symbol of knowledge.

This spell enhances the abilities of individuals to formulate and articulate their ideas. It uses an amulet that gives its wearer the power of clear communication. Feathers are used because they come from creatures of the air, and the number three is associated with the planet Mercury. Once the spell is cast, the feathers should be worn by the person who wishes to improve their powers of communication, and hung up at night over the bed.

the three-feather spell

preparation

⚹ This spell should be cast on a waxing moon, on a Wednesday, the day of Mercury. The feathers should be found rather than taken or bought, and it is unacceptable to harm a bird in order to get them. Ideal for this spell are magpie feathers, denoting discernment, owl feathers for learning, and heron feathers for creativity. If you are unable to find any of these, any feathers will do. If you do not have all the ingredients for mercury incense, use plain myrrh or dried lavender.

ingredients

⚹ A yellow candle, anointed with lavender oil. Mercury incense, made from two parts myrrh granules, one part dried dill or dill seeds, two parts dried lavender with one drop of clove oil per teaspoon dried mixture. Three bird feathers. A 6 inch (15cm) length of yellow or white sewing thread. A 12 inch (30cm) length narrow yellow ribbon or cord.

the spell

⚹ Cast a circle, welcoming the elements and lighting the element candles. Light the yellow candle, saying:

I call upon the element of air to watch over, bless and energize this spell to improve (my/friend's name) powers of communication in writing and/or speech.

✳ Sprinkle the incense on the lit charcoal disk, saying:

I call upon the powers of Mercury, swift, hot, heavenly messenger to aid me in my spell.

✳ Hold up the three feathers and say:

I invoke and honor Athena, goddess and patron of wisdom, learning and communication, to help (me/friend's name) connect ideas to action and express them with confidence and clarity.

✳ Bind the feathers together using the sewing thread, fanning them out slightly, and wind this around the shafts of the feathers until they are firmly bound and then fasten off. Holding the feathers in both hands, raise and concentrate energy into them by chanting. The chant can be sung or spoken and be of your own making, or one of the following:

Lady Athena,	Flow with the tide,	Little ones of air,
goddess of the wise,	grow with the moon,	beat your wings and fly,
star that fell to earth,	turn with the earth,	high above the earth,
from the skies.	burn like the sun.	little ones of air.

✳ You should notice the energy rising as you chant. Direct it through your voice into the feathers. Fasten the three spread feathers to the centre of the yellow ribbon or cord.

✳ Pass the finished amulet through the incense smoke, saying:

Element of air, swift Mercury, Athena, great goddess, bless this charm and she/he who wears it.

✳ With this, the spell is complete and you should wear or give the amulet to the person for whom it is intended as soon as possible.

fire magic

The element of fire is a useful ally in matters of energy, strength, inspiration, and willpower. However, some magicians are rather ambivalent about its use in magic. Some see fire as double-edged, claiming that although fire as energy or enthusiasm is part of our natural being, an overdose can start wars. However, it might equally be argued that an overdose of air makes you giddy, of water, sentimental, and none of these are true.

The Celtic Fire goddess Brighid was immensely popular in pre-Christian times. The patron saint of poets, smiths, and healers, she is often depicted as a strong, red-haired woman of fiery disposition.

This spell for confidence draws on the energies of fire, and calls on the goddess Brighid. It is an example of candle magic, which uses the physic vibes of candle colors—the energies attracted to colors because they have, over time and customary usage, become "keys" for attracting those energies—and the anointing oil in order to attract the appropriate energies. The candle used is red, for fire and for the planet Mars. When you have cast the spell, give the remainder of the nutmeg to the person for whom the spell is intended or keep it yourself, if it is for you. It can be hung over the hearth for luck.

the fire-candle spell

preparation

✳ This spell should be cast on a waxing moon, preferably on a Tuesday, day of Mars. You should use a candle that is red all the way through, rather than the color-coated type. If you can, decorate the altar or center of the circle with yellow dandelion flowers, which are dedicated to Brighid. If you cannot find all the ingredients prescribed for fire incense, use frankincense and rosemary. Similarly, if you cannot find cinnamon essential oil, steep cinnamon powder in a carrier oil for at least seven days of the waxing moon, prior to the circle.

ingredients

✳ A red candle. A teaspoon of cinnamon oil dilute. An athame or sharp bladed knife. Fire incense, made from two parts frankincense granules, one part dried rosemary, one part dried vanilla pod, one part sunflower seeds, one part marigold petals, one part freshly-grated nutmeg, with one drop of cinnamon and vanilla oil mixed in equal parts, per teaspoon dried mixture. Leave to settle for seven days prior to the spell.

the spell

✳ Cast a circle, welcoming the elements and lighting the element candles. Holding the red candle in both hands, face the fire quarter and raise it in that direction, saying:

I call upon the element of fire to watch over, bless and energize this spell to give (me/friend's name) confidence.

✳ Bring the candle back towards the altar or center of the circle and raise it, saying:

I call upon the powers of Mars the forthright, the active and the courageous to charge this spell with your energy.

✳ Still raising the candle in both hands towards the altar, or center, say:

I ask Brighid, goddess of the flames, fierce protector and breastplate of the disempowered, great inspirer and healer, to lend your fire and power to this spell.

✳ Placing the candle in a secure holder, use a few drops of cinnamon oil to anoint it top to bottom, back up again, then top to bottom once more. Chant while doing this, visualizing yourself/your friend looking happy and relaxed. The chant can be one of your own making or the traditional fire chant: We are at one with the infinite sun, forever, forever, forever.

✳ Take the athame or knife, and carve the name of the person who needs confidence vertically on the side of the candle, beginning about 7½ inches (4cm) from the wick. Holding the candle upright, carve the symbol of Mars, a circle with an arrow pointing upward to the right, above the name. Place the candle on the altar or in the center of the circle and light it, to release the energy so that the spell can do its work.

water magic

The power of water is often invoked in love spells. Its most frequent use in magic, however, is for healing. The balance aspect of water and its link to emotional issues makes it the ideal element to draw upon in cases of stress, emotional pain, or depression.

Water's association with healing is historical as well as symbolic. Ancient healing wells are found all over the British Isles, and the Roman bath and spa complexes in England indicate a long association between water and healing.

The Welsh goddess, Rhiannon, is strongly associated with the sea. The dead, who in the British Isles were seen as going into the west, over water, are said to be accompanied by Rhiannon's birds, who sing them on their way. As patron of natural justice, conciliation, and balance, Rhiannon is an ideal goddess to call upon in matters of healing.

This spell for healing is intended for someone who is sick, and is designed to send them calm, balance, and recuperation. The chant is an old witches' chant used in healing rituals. The chalice, symbol of water in the circle, is seen here as a magical cauldron with healing waters. The tumbled stones represent the three energies you will be sending, and the upturned mirror functions as a symbol of water, and to amplify the power of the spell. This spell also calls upon the energies of the moon.

the healing chalice spell

preparation

✷ This spell should be cast on a waxing moon, preferably on a Monday, day of the moon. Place the blue candle, chalice, and mirror on the altar, with the chalice on the upturned mirror. Burn healing incense, or eucalyptus or bay leaves with a little frankincense.

ingredients

✷ Healing incense, made from two parts frankincense granules, two parts mixture of equal parts peppermint, eucalyptus and bay leaves, one part apple granules or dried apple blossom, one part dried comfrey root, and one drop geranium essential oil per teaspoon dried mixture. Leave to settle for seven days prior to the spell. A blue candle, anointed with geranium oil dilute. A chalice, filled with spring water. A mirror approx 3 inches (8cm) width or diameter. Three tumbled stones, 1 inch (3cm) in circumference, one of clear quartz, one of rose quartz, and one of bloodstone. One small pouch. One cord, approx 14 feet (35cm) long.

the spell

- Cast a circle, welcoming the elements and lighting the candles. Light the blue candle, saying:

> **I call upon the element of water to watch over, and bless this spell and bring healing to (me/friend's name).**

- Hold the chalice up and say:

> **I call upon the power of the moon, pearl of the heavens, to charge this cauldron with it sacred healing powers.**

- Replace the chalice on the upturned mirror. Cup the three stones in your hands and raise them towards the altar, saying:

> **I invoke Rhiannon, goddess of the mighty waters, just and patient one, to pour healing power into this spell, to mend what is broken and heal what is hurt.**

- Keeping the stones cupped in your hand, chant the following to energize them:

> **This is the spell that I intone, flesh to flesh and bone to bone, sinew to sinew, vein to vein, may each part soon be whole again.**

- When you have raised enough energy, place the clear quartz in the chalice, saying:

> **May (I/friend's name) be calm.**

- Repeat this action with the rose quartz and bloodstone, substituting "find balance," and "recover" respectively. Leave overnight, then place them in the pouch and fasten tightly in the center of the cord. It should be worn immediately.

spirit magic

The magic used in relation to the element of spirit is for personal transformation. It is the element that most relates to our spiritual and magical selves. In spellwork, it is used less frequently than the other elements, partly because it is of more relevance to the person casting spells, than to those requesting them.

In the circle, the symbol of spirit is the cord. This is partly in imitation of the umbilical cord, which connects us with our mother before we are born. Cords appear in various rites of passage, notably initiation, when "shroud measurements" are taken. Magical patrons of the spirit element are often spider or weaving goddesses, the three Fates of Greek legend, or the Norns of Norse mythology. These goddesses spin the fates of all beings, one to spin, one to cut, and one to weave. Hecate is a good goddess for spirit spellwork as she is concerned with matters of change and continuity.

The following spell is designed to effect transformation in someone who wishes to pursue the path of witchcraft. In this spell, you will use an old charm known as a "witch's ladder," which involves tying your intention and raised energy into knots. In some spells, these knots remain tied for the duration of the spell. In this one, however, the knots are untied at a suitable juncture to release the magic to do its work.

the purple cord spell

preparation

✳ This spell should be cast on a dark moon, preferably on a Monday, day of the moon. Use a purple candle to represent spirit. If you cannot find all the ingredients prescribed for transformation incense, burn cypress oil in an oil burner.

ingredients

✳ A purple candle, anointed with cypress oil dilute. A purple cord, approximately 14 inches (35cm) long. Transformation incense, made from two parts frankincense granules, two parts myrrh, two parts sandalwood, one part dittany or mugwort, one part ground poppy seeds, one part yew berries, and one drop cypress essential oil per dessertspoon dried mixture. Leave to settle for seven days prior to the spell. A small box, to store the witch's ladder at the end of the circle.

the spell

✴ Cast a circle, welcoming the elements and lighting the element candles. Light the purple candle, saying:

> I call upon spirit, element of transformation and connection to empower this spell and bless me on my spiritual and/or magical path.

✴ Take the cord in both hands, stand before the purple candle and say:

> Hecate, mother of the night, old one, washer at the ford who prepares us for life and receives us after death, bless this cord, symbol of my spiritual journey, and guide me on the path as you guided me into life and will guide me into death.

✴ Sprinkle the incense on a lit charcoal disk, and pass the whole cord through the incense smoke to absorb its powers. Starting at the right, tie nine knots at equal spaces along the cord, saying as you do, at the appropriate knot, and fastening it on the last word of each rule:

> By rule of one, the spell's begun, by rule of two, it will hold true, by rule of three, so mote it be, by rule of four, be there no flaw, by rule of five, the spell's alive, by rule of six, the magic sticks, by rule of seven, the thing is given, by rule of eight, it will fly straight, by rule of nine, the thing is mine.

✴ Blow out the purple candle, and place it with the witch's ladder in the box. Keep both undisturbed for a full cycle of the moon. At the next dark moon, light the purple candle in a properly cast circle. Untie the knots and release the magic into the ether to begin the process of your transformation.

ninth-wave spell

Love spells are among the most frequently requested spells in the witch's repertoire. The rules and conditions for love spells, and what they can actually achieve, are very straightforward. Rule one: Magic cannot make someone fall in love with you, however much you may want them to. Rule two: No spell can focus upon attracting a particular person, as the focus of a love spell is the supplicant herself/himself. Rule three: A love spell sends out the message that the time is right for love to come to you. This final rule can be customized in a number of different ways, for example, specifying that you want someone worthy of you, but it cannot break rules one and two.

The Ninth-Wave Spell is ideal when someone is confident that they are ready for love to come into their life. You may need to ask yourself, or the person asking for a love spell, what is really needed. It could be that you do not love yourself well enough to be able to offer love just yet. In this case, a love spell to help you love yourself is ideal. Alternatively, it might be that the request for a love spell is from someone who is just plain lonely. If this is the case, a spell for finding new friends is probably more suitable.

There are a number of techniques that can be employed in love magic. It is possible to make a love philter in the form of an energized or enchanted herbal tea for the supplicant to drink. Another way of casting a love spell is to make an amulet, magically charged with your request for love to come, and worn until your new partner appears. Love oils and incenses are very popular; these use herbs, flowers, oils, and incenses associated with water, Venus, the love-planet, or are traditional love ingredients in folklore. Oils are used to anoint the body in rituals, or dropped into a magical bath to help you attract love. Be careful not to use ingredients that will irritate or burn the skin, and make sure that you dilute essential oils in the proper proportion to carrier oil. Favorite ingredients for love spells include roses, geraniums, apples, catnip, coriander, cyclamen, jasmine, marjoram, mistletoe, patchouli, and vanilla.

the ninth-wave spell

preparation
✳ This spell should be cast on a waxing moon, and on a Friday, the day ruled by Aphrodite and named for Freya; both goddesses associated with love. This spell is set on a beach shortly before the tide turns and uses the outgoing tide to carry away

your request. Ensure that you have plenty of privacy during the casting of this spell, especially when you speak the words of the spell aloud.

ingredients

✳ An outgoing tide. A stick for drawing on the sand or some pebbles to mark a circle. Three cubes of sugar.

the spell

✳ Stand a stone's throw from the water and draw a circle around you in the sand, or place pebbles around you to mark a circle. Cup the sugar cubes in your hands and say to them:

> One for the ocean for bearing my/(name)'s wish,
> one for the sweetness I send to the fish,
> one to bring sweetness to flavor my/(name)'s dish.

✳ Hold the cubes, now charged with your intention, out to sea, saying:

> Element of water, bringer of love,
> carry my/(name)'s wish out upon the ebb,
> and bring back upon the flow, within three moons, a love
> to sweeten my/(name)'s days and gladden my/(his/her)
> nights. So mote it be.

✳ Count the waves as they break on the shore and on the ninth, cast all three cubes together into the water.

✳ Step out of the circle and watch the tide wash the circle away.

✳ Within three months, love will come to you. When it does, light a blue thank you candle for the ninth wave.

mint wreath spell

Prosperity is another area that attracts lots of requests for magic. "Prosperity" is often taken to mean "more money." Although there have been cases where spells have been followed by large windfalls of money, these are the exception rather than the rule.

Witches see prosperity in a far broader sense, which incorporates money alongside other ingredients that help us to flourish and thrive. Among these are shelter, food, diet, and income. In addition, there is an element of "success" implied, which in terms of personal prosperity is defined as continual growth, happiness, and fulfillment in our lives. These two elements link together very closely, success in this sense is not possible without the material basis of sufficiency.

There are a number of traditional spells that fall into the area of prosperity; these include spells for specific objects, commercial growth, better crops, guaranteed shelter, food and warmth, and money. Various superstitions are related to this area, both modern and old. It is highly revealing of current social concerns that the majority of modern prosperity superstitions are concerned with employment. Blowing up a paper bag and bursting it "puts someone out of work," while flushing a toilet with the lid up spells layoff for someone in the household.

Of the older superstitions, charms to ensure wealth include wearing a mint leaf in your right shoe to bring money, making sure that your purse is never completely empty, and placing a coin in the hand of a newborn to ensure s/he will never be poor. These are good examples of sympathetic magic; "mint" is not only a herb, but the place where cash money is created. The herb mint also has a longtime association with prosperity spells, seen by witches and other magicians to emit powerful money-luck vibrations.

This spell uses a mint wreath as an amulet for growth and prosperity. It makes a lovely wedding or handfasting gift, or can be presented to a couple setting up home together. It should be hung in the room of the home where the most time is spent.

the mint wreath spell

preparation

✣ This spell should be cast on the night before the full moon, on a Thursday, the day ruled by Jupiter. The mint used here should, if at all possible, be either grown in your own garden, or be found growing wild. Mint is easy to grow, and is considered to be a very lucky plant to grow near your front door. There are also some attractive variegated species available, the incorporation of which would make the wreath more decorative. Plain old garden mint, however, should form the basis of the wreath. The green and purple candles should be placed on the altar or in the center prior to the casting of the circle.

ingredients

✳ A small bunch of dried sage. One green candle, anointed with almond oil. One purple candle, anointed with almond oil. At least fifty mint leaves. 7 inch (18cm) florist wire, green if possible. 24 inch (60cm) deep green satin ribbon. Three drops peppermint oil.

the spell

✳ Cast a circle, welcoming the elements and lighting the element candles. Light the sage leaves, blow out the flames and allow them to smoke. Fumigate the area completely, then extinguish.

✳ Light the green candle, saying:

> I call upon the element of earth to bless this spell for my (friend's name)'s future prosperity.

✳ Light the purple candle, saying:

> Jupiter, planet of generosity, fortune and growth, may I (friend's name) receive generosity, fortune, and growth just as I grant it to others.

✳ Thread the mint leaves near the stalk end of the leaf, onto the wire, then when it is full, shape, and fasten into a circle. Tie the green ribbon in a large bow at the bottom of the wreath. Dab the peppermint oil onto the center of the bow.

✳ Hang the wreath in the center of your home, or present it to your friends with these instructions, as soon as possible.

rag doll spell

Binding spells work by halting wrongdoers in their tracks and stopping them from causing harm. They are not "curses" designed to inflict harm, but measures taken in order to prevent it. In a sense, binding is often a kindness extended not only to those who are currently victims of unkindness and cruelty, but to the person actually inflicting the harm. They have the choice of continuing to behave badly and finding themselves obstructed in different areas of their life, or of changing their ways.

There are a number of ways to magically bind a troublemaker, the most famous being the use of a wax figure and pins. Unfortunately, this method has been misrepresented in novels and movies that depict witches using these to inflict pain or even death. Wax figures are used to symbolize a person, but the use of pins is more metaphorical. They may be used to "prick" someone's conscience or "pin down" a wrongdoer. One method of binding a troublemaker has entered our language; this involves making a tiny rag doll in the likeness of the badly behaved person and carrying it around in your pocket so that you can keep an eye on them. This is the origin of the saying that you have someone "in your pocket."

This spell expands on the theme of binding by symbolizing the harm itself as a ribbon or cord, and winding it around a doll representing the miscreant. Dolls, also known as poppets, have a long, if often misunderstood, tradition in witchcraft. They are strengthened considerably when some personal effect of the person in question goes into their making. This might be hair or a piece of their handwriting. However, what matters most is the intention with which a spell is carried out.

Don't be tempted to try to cause physical harm with a poppet. This will not work and you will have become the thing you are trying to eradicate. All that is likely to happen is that you find yourself obstructed in your own life because of your misdirected anger.

the rag doll binding spell

preparation

✴ This spell should be carried out on a waning moon, as you are diminishing someone's powers to do harm. It should be carried out on Saturday, "Saturn's day," as this planet presides over restrictions. You will be calling upon Annis, a fierce goddess who is considered to be the scourge of bullies and champion of the vulnerable.

ingredients

✴ Banishing Incense made from two parts frankincense, one part dried nettles, and one part elderberries. One black candle, anointed with rosemary oil dilute. One square of plain muslin or cotton fabric 8 inches x 4 inches (20cm x 10cm). A pen. Scissors. Black sewing thread and needle. Nettle leaves to stuff a small doll, approximately 4 inches x 4 inches (10cm x 10cm). Two small buttons. Water. 24 inches (60cm) black cord or ribbon.

the spell

✴ Cast a circle, welcoming the elements and lighting the element candles. Sprinkle incense on the lit charcoal disk. Light the black candle, saying:

> **Annis, goddess of the traveling people, fierce in protection and just in return bless this spell to bind (name of miscreant) from doing harm.**

✴ Fold the muslin in half to form a square, draw a human outline on one side and cut around it through the doubled fabric. Sew the two pieces of cloth together, beginning at the neck, going around the body to the other side of the neck. Leave the head open. Turn the figure inside out, stuff with nettles then sew the head up and add the buttons as eyes. Hold the doll above the altar or center of the circle, saying:

> **I name thee (name of miscreant).**

✴ Sprinkle the doll with water, and pass through the incense. Pass the cord through the incense, saying:

> **I name thee as (miscreant's name)'s harmful behavior.**

✴ Wind the cord tightly around the doll, repeat these words until there is only enough cord to fasten it firmly:

> **I bind you, I hinder you, I halt you.**

✴ Burn or bury the doll after the circle to confirm the spell and make it irreversible.

rowan cross spell

Luck is one of life's great puzzles. Our perception of it is often colored by our personal circumstances. For someone poor, living hand to mouth, finding a few coins might be considered "lucky." Someone who has lost them, however, may consider the very same event as "unlucky" for them.

Some forms of luck magic are designed to keep bad luck away, implying that absence of misfortune is "lucky" in itself. Talismans to fend off bad luck are very common, and most of them have ancient origins. One of the oldest still in existence is the use of eye imagery to repel bad wishing. Ironically, being "overlooked" by someone wishing you harm was also known as the "evil eye," so the use of eyes painted over doorways, or glass eyes worn around the person to deflect harm, is a form of fighting like with like. This belief originates from ancient Egypt, where the eye of Horus was believed to repel all evil.

Other talismans include the carrying or hanging in the house of herbs or twigs known for their protective properties. Broom, rosemary, and lavender can be carried or worn, hung over the hearth, or grown by the front door for protection. Some, like clover, rowan berries, and wood, combine to bring the wearer protection and luck.

Sometimes, things that come to us through chance are considered to be very lucky, for example, finding a four-leafed clover. Other things received directly from the sky, such as leaves falling from trees or feathers from birds, if caught before they land, are supposed to bring good luck to the catcher.

The following spell uses wood from the rowan tree. The rowan has the reputation of keeping harm from the door. Rowan wood is also considered lucky, and an amulet made from it is reputed to bring the wearer good luck. Its berries can be strung in a circle to bring good health, and its wood burned in protection and luck incenses.

the rowan cross spell

preparation

※ This spell should be cast on a waxing moon, to draw good luck. Sunday, day of smiling fortune, is the best day to cast. If there are no fallen twigs available, you should cut some from the tree, but remember to leave a gift of wine-soaked bread and a small coin buried in the earth near its roots. You will call upon the goddess Fortuna, whose symbol is the wheel, which resembles the amulet you are going to make.

ingredients

✴ Oil burner. Blend of equal parts rosemary, cinnamon, and benzoin essential oils. One gold or orange candle anointed with the above blend, diluted. One purple candle. Two pieces rowan twig, 5 inches (2cm) in length if to be worn or carried, 3 inches (8cm) if to be hung in the house. A ball of red wool.

the spell

✴ Cast a circle, welcoming the elements and lighting the element candles. Light the oil burner to release the scent and vibrations of the oil blend. Light the yellow candle, saying:

> I welcome the Sun,
> may it shine on my charm,
> bring forth fortune and health,
> and protect me (friend's name) from harm.

✴ Light the purple candle, saying:

> Fortuna, Fortuna,
> goddess of the wheel,
> may the sun of fortune burn,
> as the wheel of fortune turns.

✴ Take the rowan twigs and fasten them in the shape of an equal-armed (solar) cross, binding this tightly with the red wool.

✴ Continue to weave the wool around the crossarms, winding around each twig and across to the next spoke. Stretch wool across the gaps between the spoke, until the cross is covered with woven wool to halfway along the arm lengths from the center.

✴ This rowan cross should be either carried on the person, worn as a pendant, or hung in the house to bring good luck.

yellow letter spell

Success in the way the world generally sees it usually depends on a mixture of your own abilities, efforts, and a little bit of luck. Success in your chosen career, your school or college work, or in getting a promotion or a job, may be dependent upon all of these factors.

It should be recognized that discrimination and disadvantage can offer obstacles to your potential achievement. Discrimination can be challenged. It is an issue that everyone needs to work against, but casting a spell is not the correct way of dealing with it.

Working to study or improve your abilities to meet the criteria of a new job, pass an exam, or win a promotion are necessary before you apply for the new post, or enter an exam. Magic will not get you through an exam you have not studied for nor win you a promotion you do not deserve. Spells for success are based, therefore, on the understanding that you have already met the necessary criteria. "Success" spells in this area are actually communication spells, which use the element of air and the planetary influence of Mercury to facilitate in areas of education, commerce, and employment.

The Yellow Letter Spell is a combination of magic and autosuggestion. Sending yourself a letter to inform yourself that the success you wish for is within your grasp, is a mixture of self-affirmation, and a message to the magical web. It signifies to the web that you intend to be successful while psychologically reinforcing those intentions within you.

the yellow letter spell

preparation
✴ This spell should be carried out on a waxing moon to draw success toward you. It should be cast on Wednesday, the day of Mercury. You will be calling on Helen of the Ways, a Welsh deity who is the patron of travelers. She is a champion of those trying to make progress in their lives.

ingredients
✴ A yellow candle anointed with lavender oil. Success incense made from equal parts of cinnamon, benzoin, and frankincense, with a little lemon zest added. A quill pen or ordinary pen with a large feather attached. A yellow envelope and a sheet of writing paper. An express postage stamp (first class).

the spell

✴ Cast a circle, welcoming the elements and lighting the element candles. Light the yellow candle, saying:

> I call upon the powers of Mercury the swift and sure to carry my message into the Ether and bring success and my letter, back to me.

✴ Sprinkle the incense on the lit charcoal disk, and visualize a woman, dressed in yellow, sitting at a gate by a path, in the air quarter. Speak to her, saying:

> Helen of the Ways, gatekeeper and goddess of the wayside, bless this traveler on her/his journey and bring her/him safely to success. Blessed Be.

✴ Take the pen and write a short letter to yourself, confirming that you will have the success you wish yourself. It should be direct and simple such as:

Dear Ann-Marie,
I am writing to confirm that you will succeed in your chosen career/course of study/application for promotion.
Yours sincerely,
Ann-Marie Gallagher

✴ Fold the letter and put it into the envelope. Address it to yourself, and on the reverse, where the envelope is sealed, draw the symbol for Mercury (Venus/female sign with horns on top). Place the postage stamp on the envelope, and stamping it on firmly with your fist, say loudly:

> So mote it be!

✴ Mail the letter as soon as possible. When you receive it, open it, read it and put it in a spell box or other safe place until you pass the exam/get the job/receive the promotion, then burn it.

potpourri spell

There is a saying that we can choose our friends, but not our families. This can probably be extended to include colleagues at school, college, workplace, and roommates. If the atmosphere at home, at school, college, or in work is unpleasant, there are lots of witchcraft traditions you can draw on to sweeten the situation a little.

One way is to use a floral remedy. One of the best flowers to place in the center of a home or office with a bad atmosphere is the sweet pea, whose curling vines signify harmony. Its pleasant scent encourages amity and cheerfulness. Another good flower to encourage harmony is the daisy. Its relationship to the sun draws out the sunnier side of people's natures, and the daisy chain is an excellent symbol of togetherness.

Chamomile is well known for its restorative and calming properties. If you cannot cultivate some in a pot in the home or office, a bowl of dried flower heads will help settle the atmosphere wherever it is placed. Burning calming, harmonizing oils can also have a relaxing effect on the people around you. Geranium, lavender, and chamomile are the best oils to use. You should check, however, that none of your college or work friends or roommates are pregnant or have high blood pressure, as some essential oils cause physiological reactions that can be harmful for these conditions.

Another way of creating harmony is to place bowls of orange-colored fruit in the heart of the space concerned. Satsumas and oranges are ideal. Sharing fruit around can be a good bonding gesture, and the bright colors cheer up the work environment.

The Potpourri Spell draws upon the properties of plants and herbs as well as the sympathetic magical act of mixing to induce harmony. Sunflowers and marigolds are included for their sunny aspects. Chamomile, vanilla, sandalwood, and cloves are noted for their harmonious vibrations; the dried orange, tangerine peel, and orange oil are used for their calming influence; and the cinnamon and clove oils for their warming aspect.

the potpourri spell

preparation
✴ This spell should be cast on a waxing moon to make harmony grow. The ideal day is a Friday, day of Venus. You will be requesting the help of Aphrodite, in her aspect as peacemaker and patron of friendship. Her symbol here is the scallop shell.

ingredients

✴ A pink candle anointed with geranium oil dilute. A handful of sandalwood shavings. A handful of mixed orange and/or satsuma peel, dried in the microwave or over a radiator. A handful of dried chamomile flowers. A large bowl, and if possible, a mortar and pestle for mixing. A handful of dried sunflowers. A handful of dried marigold petals. Five large vanilla pods. Nine drops each of cinnamon, clove, and orange essential oils. A large half scallop shell. A large square of muslin to cover the bowl.

the spell

✴ Cast a circle, welcoming the elements and lighting the element candles. Light the pink candle saying:

> **I ask for the aid of Aphrodite, lovely goddess of harmony and peace, in bringing harmony to my/(name)'s workplace/classroom/home.**

✴ Blend the shavings, peel, and chamomile flowers together in a mortar. Transfer this to the large bowl and blend all other ingredients, using the shell as a spoon to mix them all together, chanting as you do:

> **As I mix this magic blend,**
> **enmity and conflict end.**

✴ As you are chanting and mixing, visualize the people in question in the situation you encounter them, smiling, shaking hands, and helping each other. Cover with muslin and leave on the altar overnight.

✴ Transfer the potpourri mixture to a large, decorative bowl at the center or in a prominent place in the home/office/study or classroom as appropriate.

the magical web

Now that you have worked your way through this book, and participated in the exercises and activities, you will have a much better idea of who and what witches are. Experiencing something for yourself is worth one hundred descriptions in terms of understanding and knowledge. Your experiences in the inner journeys, outward activities, and spell-casting described in this book will hopefully have provided you with a much clearer understanding of magic and witchcraft generally. They will also have given you a better idea of what is meant by a "spiritual path," and of your place on your own, individual spirit web.

identifying yourself

You will have noted that there are a number of ways in which you might now identify yourself. Are you happy to describe yourself, or have yourself described as a witch? Or are you more comfortable with the term "pagan" to describe your spirituality? You may find yourself drawn toward one or another of the paths of witchcraft described in this book—either through your politics, personal experiences, or preferences. This may lead you to work with other, like-minded people, or you may find that the path you choose is that of the hedgewitch, or solitary, who prefers to work alone. It could be that you are happier thinking of yourself as a magician who works with the tides and cycles of nature, celebrating the changes in the passing year, and drawing upon these spiritually to source your magical abilities.

harm none

Whatever, and whoever you decide you are, you will need to consider your position in relation to that of others. As you have already learned, the great web of being links us all,

Are you happy to describe yourself, or have yourself described as a witch? Or are you more comfortable with the term "pagan?"

and includes our nonhuman relations, such as animals, rocks, and trees. Your position in the web is your personal, individual discovery, but its impact is not on you alone; it affects the whole web. If you consider that every one of our actions reverberates along the strands that bind us all together, you will realize the importance of leading a responsible, ethical way of life. The admonition to "harm none" is almost impossible to follow in a pure sense; for example, crossing a field crushes the grass. Common sense, the mainspring of wisdom in witchcraft, tells us that the Wiccan Rede is intended to make us stop and think about our actions, and to consider who or what might be harmed by them. The first part of the Rede advises: "Do thy will an it harm none." This is an invitation to dare to be different, and to fly in the face of convention if convention is leading us to act stupidly or harmfully. The tag on the end warns us, however, that we must always consider the consequences of what we do, how we act, and what we say; not just upon ourselves, but also upon others.

the greater impact

If you do decide that what you are is a witch, consider the impact that this will have on your life and on those around you. It could be that some people profess themselves hurt or disappointed that you have chosen this path. This is more likely to happen if they do not

More important, always consider your position in the wider web, and practice asking yourself the following questions: "What am I doing that makes a difference? What am I doing to challenge what is harmful?"

understand what being a witch actually involves. If these are people close to you, you will probably want them to understand that you have not been "sucked in" by a weird cult, but are making a choice that is responsible and right for you. It could be that this takes time, and that there will be some resistance to this, because of the legacy of prejudice and misunderstanding that, to a certain extent, still persists. Another likely reaction is that people are positive, but then imagine you have all sorts of miraculous powers and overwhelm you with requests for help, advice, and spells. Educating people takes time and energy, and you will have to decide which people are most worth educating, and which are just going to drain you. One way of helping people understand your decision is to give them this book to read. Another way is to reassure them by example; live your life according to the spiritual and magical ethics of the Craft by way of demonstration.

making a difference

Whatever you decide to be your future, remember that it is not set in stone, and changing your mind about the flavor, methods, and mode of identification you choose is allowed. More important, always consider your position in the wider web, and practice asking yourself the following questions: "What am I doing that makes a difference? What am I doing to challenge what is harmful?" If you do this, you go with blessings and walk in light.

Blessed Be.

index

acknowledgments

Thank you all at Mitchell Beazley, and Barron's, who have helped develop this project, especially Vivien Antwi and Michelle Bernard. Many thanks to Liz Puttick, my friend and agent, for her encouragement and to my friends and colleagues Harper, Jayne Ovens, Heather Ainscough, Debbie Bentley, and Cathy Lubelska. Thanks are due to those students and colleagues at the University of Central Lancashire who offered their support and interest. To my young friends Mica, Michael, Mitchell, Drew, Darrell, Rebecca, and Sam, thank you for asking all the questions that made writing this easier. I offer my gratitude to Ann and Heather of the Women's Dome for allowing me to develop workshops in witchcraft and magic at the Big Green Gathering Festival year on year, and similar thanks go out to Catherine of the Northern Green Gathering, to the Oakleaf Circle, and to the Preston Moot. A big thank you to my ever-patient children, Michelle, Chantal, and Matthew, and to Tony the Outlaw. The biggest thanks of all goes to my wonderful partner, Steve Turner, for the unerring support which has enabled me to write this book.

bibliography

Adams, C (ed), *Ecofeminism and the Sacred*, Continuum, New York, 1993.

Aldridge, A, *Religion in the Contemporary World: A Sociological Introduction*, Polity, Oxford, 2000.

Allen, A, *A Dictionary of Sussex Folk Medicine*, Countryside Books, Newbury, Berks, 1995.

Anderson, L (ed), *Sisters of the Earth*, Vintage Books, New York, 1991.

Ankarloo, B and Henningsen, G (eds), *Early Modern European Witchcraft: Centres and Peripheries*, Clarendon Press, Oxford, 1990.

Billington, S and Green, M, *The Concept of the Goddess*, Routledge, London, 1996.

Carr-Gomm, P, *The Druid Renaissance*, Thorsons, London, 1996.

Christ, C P and Plaskow, J (eds), *Womanspirit Rising: A Feminist Reader in Religion*, Harper Collins, San Francisco, 1992.

Crowley, V, *Wicca: The Old Religion in the New Age*, Aquarian Press, London, 1989.

Ehrenreich, B and English, D, *Witches, Midwives, and Nurses: A History of Women Healers*, Feminist Press, New York, 1973.

Ellis-Davidson, H, *Roles of the Northern Goddess*, Routledge, London, 1998.

Estes, C P, *Women Who Run with the Wolves: Contacting the Power of the Wild Woman*, Rider, London, 1994.

Ginzburg, C, *Ecstasies: Deciphering the Witches' Sabbath*, Hutchinson Radius, London, 1990.

Griffin, W (ed), *Daughters of the Goddess: Studies of Healing, Identity, and Empowerment*, AltaMira, New York, 2000.

Guest, C (translator), *The Mabinogion*, Dent & Sons Ltd, London, 1961.

Harvey G, *Listening People, Speaking Earth: Contemporary Paganism*, Hurst & Company, London, 1997.

Harvey, G and Hardman, C, *Paganism Today*, Thorsons, London, 1996.

Hester, M, *Lewd Women and Wicked Witches: A Study of the Dynamics of Male Domination*, Routledge, London, 1992.

Hirshfield, J, *Women in Praise of the Sacred: 43 Centuries of Spiritual Poetry by Women*, HarperCollins, New York, 1994.

Hopkins, M, *The Discovery of Witches*, London, 1647, 1928.

Hutton, R, *The Stations of the Sun: A History of the Ritual Year in Britain*, Oxford University Press, Oxford, 1997.

Kennett, F, *Folk Medicine: Fact and Fiction*, Marshall Cavendish, London, 1984.

Kramer, H and Sprenger, J (T M Summers), *Malleus Maleficarum*, 1486, 1928.

Larner, Christina, *Enemies of God: The Witch-hunt in Scotland*, Chatto & Windus, London, 1981.

Larrington, C (ed), *The Feminist Companion to Mythology*, Pandora, London, 1992.

Levack, B P, *The Witch-Hunt in Early Modern Europe*, Longman, London, 1987.

Llewellyn-Barstow, A, *Witchcraze: A New History of the European Witch Hunts*, Pandora, San Francisco, 1994.

Martin, R, *Witchcraft and the Inquisition in Venice 1550-1650*, Blackwell, Oxford, 1989.

Mountainwater, S, *Ariadne's Thread: A Workbook of Goddess Magic*, The Crossing Press, Freedom, 1996.

Pearson, J, Roberts, R and Samuel, G, *Nature Religion Today: Paganism in the Modern World*, Edinburgh University Press, Edinburgh, 1998.

Pickering, D, *Dictionary of Witchcraft*, Cassell, London, 1996.

Potts, T H, "Discovery of witchcraft in the county of Lancaster", Lancashire Records Office: pamphlet, 1613.

Puttick, E, *Women in New Religions: In Search of Community, Sexuality and Spiritual Power*, MacMillan, London, 1997.

Richards, J, *Sex, Dissidence and Damnation: Minority Groups in the Middle Ages*, Routledge, London, 1992.

Rutherford, W, *Celtic Mythology: The Nature and Influence of Celtic Myth — From Druidism to Arthurian Legend*, Thorsons, London, 1995.

Scot, R, *The Discoverie of Witchcraft*, York: E.P. Publishing, 1584, 1886, 19-.

Spretnak, C, *Lost Goddesses of Early Greece: A Collection of Pre-Hellenic Myths*, Beacon Press, Boston, 1984.

Starhawk, M Macha Nightmare, and The Reclaiming Collective, *The Pagan Book of Living and Dying*, HarperSanFrancisco, San Francisco, 1997.

Wood, J, *The Celtic Book of Living and Dying*, Duncan Baird, London, 2000.

picture credits